Chocolate

Handmade chocolate Easter eggs

Sverre Sætre

Chocolate

Co-author: Hanne Hay Sætre

Photographs by Christian Brun

BONNIER
BOOKS

Thanks to

Eyvind Hellstrøm, Bagatelle Restaurant
for the foreword

Restaurant Bølgen of Moi on Høvikodden
for lending me their kitchen

Riise & GG Storkjøkken AS
for lending equipment

Gastronaut AS
for lending equipment

© J.W. Cappelens Forlag a·s 2004
Original published in Norway under the
title 'Sverres Sjokolade' by Cappelen in 2004.
First published in 2008 in English by Bonnier Books,
Appledram Barns, Birdham Road, Chichester, PO20 7EQ.
www.bonnierbooks.co.uk

ISBN 978-1-905825-57-8

Recipes using raw or very lightly cooked eggs should be avoided by infants, the elderly, pregnant women, convalescents, and anyone with a chronic condition.

English translation by Rae Walter for First Edition Translations Ltd, Cambridge, UK
Edited by JMS Books llp

Printed in China

Degree of difficulty
The squares indicate the degree of difficulty of each recipe and help you to estimate preparation time. One square means you can make it in a relatively short time, whereas four squares mean you should start preparing the day before. This applies to most of the recipes, but there are a few exceptions such as parfaits and ices, which are quick to make but you must of course reckon on a few hours for freezing before they can be served. Use the squares as an indication, and always read through the recipe carefully before you start.

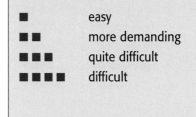

■   easy
■ ■   more demanding
■ ■ ■   quite difficult
■ ■ ■ ■   difficult

Contents

Dancer sculpted in chocolate, Nordic Confectioners' Competition

Chocoholic

Chocolate is well known as a stimulating aphrodisiac, a tonic and a good source of nourishment. It alleviates stress, anxiety, fatigue and depression, but you can just eat it for sheer enjoyment. In moderation it is good for us humans, but it is not good for animals, so no treats for the dog!

Chocoholic connoisseurs will immediately recognise a splendid, real, dark chocolate and pounce on it greedily. Sverre Sætre is one such person but he is also a professional. His chocolate sculptures mark the glittering stages in what is already a long career, despite his relative youth. Those who have seen his figures, forms and profiles may well feel that they should be displayed in art galleries and exhibitions instead of being consumed with relish.

Sverre wields his spatula like a surgeon. He uses his scales with precision and beats eggs with great gusto to conjure up the sheen in a chocolate zabaglione or the brilliance in the covering – couverture, as it is known – in little mouthfuls of chocolate, making them irresistibly appetising. Sverre's chocomania is really all about transforming the true, pure, delicious taste of cocoa beans into smooth velvet in the mouth. Sweet, factory-made chocolate and popular, mass-market filled bars really annoy him and he would never touch one.

Sverre's chocolate world looks different. It is bittersweet. It starts with cocoa beans from the best cocoa-producing countries – Brazil, Ecuador and Venezuela. In Europe, the cocoa beans are turned into blocks of chocolate with a cocoa mass content of anything from 40 to 72 and even up to 85%. The rest is cocoa butter and sweetener.

After that, the artist is free to take the rough block and transform it into small edible jewels – mousses, marquises, charlottes, millefeuilles, truffles, parfaits, soufflés or delices – light, dark, milk or ivory.

When Sverre speaks about chocolate, his language is both specialised and lyrical, but when he talks about these delicacies in his local dialect, it suddenly becomes much more down to earth.

This book should be bedtime reading for all chocoholics; it will certainly cause you to have some delightful bittersweet, white and dark dreams, after which you can wake up to a new day and discuss whether chocolate is best enjoyed with milk, coffee, coconut, mint, hazelnuts and almonds or orange, wine vinegar, whisky or pepper.

Whichever you prefer, Sverre Sætre's book about these dark beans from South America will surely inspire you to melt bars of chocolate over low heat, add the recommended ingredients and delight your nearest and dearest with a home-made work of art for sheer pleasure.

Chocolatissimo!
Eyvind Hellstrøm

Cakes, confectionery and sculptures

When I was at cookery school, I came across an article about the Norwegian national cooking team. They were preparing for the Culinary Olympics, and among other things in the article was a picture of the confectioner Lars Lian, who was working on a beautiful chocolate sculpture. I was absolutely fascinated and went straight off to Erichsen's Konditori in Trondheim to have a closer look at the place. In the same year, I got a summer job with Lars Lian. He gave me an insight into the art of confectionery and how chocolate can be used. My interest in chocolate had been aroused.

In the autumn of that year I went to Oslo and started as an apprentice with Eyvind Hellstrøm at the restaurant Bagatelle. There I learned to compile menus, make fish and meat dishes and work with the most fantastic raw materials. Nevertheless, I was happiest with desserts, and I decided to specialise in making sweet dishes. After finishing my apprenticeship and working for a time as a chef, I returned to Trondheim and started an apprenticeship with Lars Lian.

The raw material that interested me most was chocolate. I spent most of my spare time researching the special properties of chocolate and finding out how to handle it in order to shape it the way I wanted. I soon discovered that chocolate is unique, and that I could use it like an artist's material in many ways. Chocolate can be carved, moulded, turned on a lathe and modelled. The possibilities are only limited by the imagination.

Another thing that fascinated me about chocolate was that there are many different kinds. Chocolate actually has a lot in common with wine, because the taste varies according to the type of cocoa bean, how the beans are grown and the way the production process is carried out. I taught myself to distinguish between the different types and assess them according to smell and taste, tanning agent content and so on. At the same time, I began to read about chocolate and discovered that it has an amazingly interesting history, starting with the Mayas in South America.

My interest in chocolate began with a news item about the Norwegian national cooking team, and by 2004, I was actually a member of the national cooking team creating sculptures in chocolate for the autumn Culinary Olympics.

In this book I would love to share my knowledge and experience of chocolate with you and to pass on some of my favourite recipes, which have given pleasure to me and to others over the years.

Sverre Sætre

About chocolate

From beans to chocolate

Theobroma cacao is the scientific name for the cocoa tree. The name comes from the Greek word 'theobroma', meaning food of the gods, and the Aztec 'cacahoatl', meaning cocoa. The cocoa tree does not thrive in direct sunlight, so it grows in the shade of other trees. It needs heat and humidity and flourishes best in the rain forest between 21 and 22 degrees latitude. It used to grow only in South America, but now it is cultivated throughout the equatorial zone.

The cocoa tree produces fruit about 15–30 cm long and 7–8 cm wide. The fruits contain succulent white flesh and about 40 seeds, the cocoa beans. It is these beans that are eventually made into chocolate.

There are three main types of cocoa bean: criollo, forastero and trinitario. Hybrids of these can also be found. The best beans are criollo, but they only constitute about 10% of total production. The forastero bean is considered to be the least good of the three types. Trinitario is a cross between criollo and forastero and came into existence during a storm. The hybridisation was the work of nature. The trinitario bean is considered to be of medium quality in relation to the other main types, and makes up about 20% of world production.

There are many reasons for the variations in the quality of chocolate, not least because there are a large number of stages in between the cocoa bean and the finished chocolate. There are also differences in the beans used and where they are grown. Read on to find out about how chocolate is manufactured. We will also explain what distinguishes quality chocolate from chocolate that is produced with maximum profit in mind.

Harvesting

Cocoa fruits are harvested all the year round, but the most important seasons are March–May and October–November. The cocoa farmers use machetes to cut down the fruits, then they split them open and remove the beans. The cocoa beans are placed in small raffia boxes and covered with banana leaves to prevent them from drying out.

Fermenting

After harvesting, the cocoa beans must go through a fermentation process. The boxes are left to stand for 4–8 days so the beans can acquire their full flavour. Cocoa beans contain over 550 aromatic molecules, which develop flavours and aromas during fermentation.

Drying

After fermentation, the husks are removed from the beans and laid out to dry on rush mats. Ideally, the water content of the beans should be reduced from around 50% to 5–7%. The cocoa workers turn the beans several times a day so they all get the same amount of sun. The drying process takes 6–10 days, depending on the strength of the sun. By the time the beans have finished drying, they have turned brown, the aroma has developed and the fat content – or cocoa butter – amounts to almost 50%.

Sorting

Now the beans are sorted according to quality. The poorest beans, which are flat and small, are used for cocoa butter and cocoa powder. The fine big beans go to the chocolate manufacturers. The price of the beans is determined by the major stock exchanges. Almost all the cocoa beans from Central and South America are sold on the New York Stock Exchange, while cocoa beans from Africa and South-East Asia are sold through London.

Roasting

At the chocolate factory, the beans are roasted at a temperature of 80–150 °C. The combination of temperature and the length of time the beans are roasted vary between manufacturers, and also take account of the type and quality of the beans. Great care is taken to ensure that each batch is roasted separately to give the beans the best possible opportunity to achieve their full potential. After that, beans from different batches can be mixed to give the exact blend required.

Chocolate production can be compared with winemaking. Winemakers have tasters, whose job is to test the quality of the grapes every day. Chocolate manufacturers also have tasters who test and assess the beans.

Milling

After roasting the beans are shelled and then crushed and ground. This must be done with great care in order to get the best out of the beans. They have to be ground down very fine to a particle size of 17–19 microns (1 micron = 1 millionth of a metre). This takes about 24 hours. Our tongues can begin to distinguish particles when they are over 20 microns in size, so we can safely say 'fine-ground'.

Blending

After milling, the finely ground beans are mixed with sugar, vanilla and emulsifier. At the start, the cocoa mass contains about 50% cocoa butter, but extra cocoa butter is added during this process to improve the consistency and melting properties of the chocolate. Most producers add a little lecithin, an emulsifier made from soya beans. Soya lecithin is used to bind the chocolate solids together.

Manufacturers more concerned with profit than quality replace genuine vanilla with vanillin, a cheap chemically produced substance based on waste products from the cellulose industry. The result is not at all good. Many manufacturers even replace cocoa butter with cheaper hardened vegetable fats, which are not only bad for the health but also give the chocolate a poorer flavour and alter its properties.

Chocolate Easter eggs

Conching

Finally the chocolate is tipped into a drum, where it is kept constantly in motion for 1–5 days at a temperature of 47–53 °C. The main purpose of this is to mix the ingredients together thoroughly in order to achieve a fine, smooth chocolate mass. In addition, the acids in the chocolate must be released, as chocolate has a very high acid content; without conching it would be bitter and completely inedible.

Tempering

This is the final stage in the processing of chocolate. This process helps the fat crystals in the liquid chocolate to collect so that it hardens quickly and looks even and shiny. The chocolate is moulded into slabs or pellets. Chocolate that does not go through this process looks grey and hardens slowly. You can see an example of this if you look at chocolate that has melted, for instance in the sun. When it hardens again it looks grey and old. If it is tempered again, it regains its colour and sheen. This tempering process is described on page 14.

There are many stages in the production process as outlined above, and at each stage cuts can be made to reduce production costs.

What real chocolate should contain
Dark chocolate: cocoa mass, cocoa butter, sugar, vanilla and emulsifier (soya lecithin)
Milk chocolate: cocoa mass, cocoa butter, sugar, dried milk, vanilla and emulsifier (soya lecithin)
White chocolate: cocoa butter, sugar, vanilla and emulsifier (soya lecithin)

Cocoa butter is the world's most expensive fat. In addition to demand from the food industry, it is used extensively in the cosmetic and pharmaceutical industries. Many manufacturers substitute the expensive cocoa butter with other, cheaper vegetable fats. Non-temp chocolate is the designation for chocolate in which cocoa butter has been replaced by other fats. This chocolate does not have the same properties as chocolate that contains cocoa butter and the taste and consistency are nothing like as good.

Cocoa mass content
Essential information for anyone who wants to work with chocolate
For recipes containing chocolate it is vital to take the cocoa mass content of the chocolate as a starting point. The list of contents states what percentage of cocoa mass the chocolate contains.

Cocoa mass = cocoa + cocoa butter

The proportion of cocoa butter to cocoa in any chocolate varies, but there is usually slightly more cocoa butter than cocoa. In a chocolate with 70% cocoa mass there is around 40% cocoa butter and 30%

cocoa powder. The rest is mainly sugar, except for 1% emulsifier and vanilla.

It is important to check this when choosing chocolate for recipes. The cocoa mass percentage is always stated in the declaration of contents. Many manufacturers also give the percentage contained in the chocolate on the front of the packaging.

Recently there has been a great deal of focus on the idea that dark chocolate with a high cocoa mass content has healthy properties. You should therefore be aware that a number of manufacturers show a higher percentage on the front of the pack than the actual total in the chocolate. In Norway, the law obliges manufacturers to declare the cocoa mass content in the chocolate coating, but they do not have to declare the cocoa mass content in the filling. That is fine if the filling is marzipan, but if the filling is also dark chocolate, it can be difficult to see the difference between the filling and the coating and you may be tempted to believe that all the chocolate contains the percentage stated on the front.

If you use it as 70%, for example in a recipe for chocolate mousse, the mousse will not set as it should and it will also be too sweet, so the result will not be a success.

In my own recipes, I prefer to use a French brand of chocolate called Valrhona. This manufacturer does its utmost to make good chocolate, from the cocoa bean to the finished product.

In 100 grams of chocolate with a cocoa mass content of 50%, there are 50 grams of cocoa mass and 50 grams of sugar. In a chocolate with a 70% cocoa mass content, there are 70 grams of cocoa mass and 30 grams of sugar. If you use chocolate with a 50% cocoa mass content in a recipe based on chocolate with a 70% cocoa mass content, the end product will be too sweet and will not contain sufficient cocoa butter to give the right consistency.

The recipes in this book list chocolate with a specific percentage of cocoa mass. But don't worry

Wedding cake in chocolate. © Studio Dreyer & Hensley AS

too much. You can use any chocolate for the recipes as long as you take account of the quantity of sugar in proportion to the cocoa mass content. It is not very difficult.

We can use this recipe for chocolate mousse as an example:

3 egg yolks (60 g)
40 g sugar
40 ml + 230 ml whipping cream (38% fat)
125 g dark chocolate with 70% cocoa mass

If you want to use a chocolate with 60% cocoa mass in a recipe worked out on the basis of 70% chocolate, proceed as follows: multiply the number of grams of chocolate, i.e. 125, by 70 (percentage content of the chocolate in the recipe) and divide by 60 (percentage content of your chocolate).

The answer is 145.83 grams, which we round up to 146 grams. This means that we must use 146 grams of chocolate with 60% cocoa mass.

Now we have added more chocolate than there would have been originally. As a 60% chocolate contains more sugar than one with 70%, we have automatically added more sugar. We have to subtract this from the quantity of sugar given in the recipe, so we take the 146 grams of chocolate and subtract the original 125 grams, which leaves 21 grams. This means that we must use 21 grams less sugar than given in the recipe. In the chocolate mousse recipe, this is 40 grams. 40 grams minus 21 grams = 19 grams, so we must use 146 grams of chocolate and 19 grams of sugar. The proportions will then be correct and the result will be perfect.

   If it is the other way around, and the recipe is based on chocolate with 60% cocoa mass and the chocolate we have is 70%, we have to put in less

chocolate and more sugar than it says in the recipe. The calculation is as follows: multiply the number of grams of chocolate in the recipe, i.e. 146 grams if we keep to the same chocolate mousse recipe, by 60 (percentage content of the chocolate in the recipe) and divide by 70 (percentage content in the chocolate we have). The answer is 125 grams of chocolate. 146 grams of chocolate minus 125 grams = 21 grams, which means that we must increase the quantity of sugar by 21 grams. The 19 grams of sugar in the recipe plus 21 grams = 40 grams.

Tempering chocolate

If chocolate is to be used for things like dipping biscuits, coating sweets and making various kinds of chocolate decoration, it is important that is goes through a process known as tempering. To obtain a smooth, shiny chocolate, you need to master the art of tempering. It is not disastrous if you do not succeed every time, as the chocolate can be melted and used again.

   When tempering chocolate, it is important to have a good thermometer that measures from 25 to 85 °C. It is difficult to specify the quantity of chocolate, but it is easier to achieve a successful result with a relatively large portion than with a small one. Use a minimum of 300 grams. Any leftovers can be saved and tempered again on another occasion. It is worth using chocolate with a relatively high cocoa butter content. Dark chocolate with less than 50% cocoa mass contains too little cocoa butter and does not melt nicely. It becomes viscous and unsuitable for the job.

There are two ways of tempering chocolate:

Method A
1. Finely chop the chocolate and melt it in a bain-marie over low heat or in a microwave oven,

see page 19. When fully melted, the temperature of dark chocolate should be 55 °C, milk chocolate 45–50 °C and white chocolate 43–45 °C.

2. When the chocolate reaches the temperature given above, pour it onto a slab of polished stone (a marble slab is ideal). For rapid cooling, 'table' the chocolate. Use a palette knife to spread out the chocolate mass, then scrape it back into the middle. By then the temperature should have fallen to 28 °C for dark chocolate and 27–28 °C for white and milk chocolate.

3. When the temperature of the chocolate mass has fallen to the required amount, pour it back into the bowl and warm it up to 31–32 °C for dark chocolate, 29–30 °C for milk chocolate or 29 °C for white. This is the 'working temperature'; if it falls, warm it up once more.

Chocolate can be carefully warmed up again in a bain-marie or a microwave. Or you can do as I do and use a heat gun or a hair dryer (!) and carefully warm the chocolate, stirring all the time. When the heat source is turned off, all additional heat is immediately cut off and the chocolate does not get any warmer, whereas, if you use a bain-marie, you have to remember that the bowl remains warm and gives off quite a lot of heat even after it is removed from the hot water. This may result in the chocolate becoming hotter than the desired temperature, and then you will have to start all over again.

When the chocolate reaches the desired temperature, test to check if it is properly tempered. Stick the point of a knife into the chocolate and put it in the refrigerator for a minute. If the chocolate is correctly tempered, it will have begun to set with a uniform colour.

Method B
A quicker way of tempering chocolate that also gives a good result.

1. Finely chop the chocolate and melt half of it in a bain-marie or a microwave, see page 19. Dark chocolate should be heated to 55 °C, milk chocolate to 45–50 °C and white chocolate to 43–45 °C.

2. Remove the bowl of melted chocolate from the bain-marie and gradually add the other half of the finely chopped chocolate, stirring all the time. Use a plastic spoon to stir until all the chocolate has melted. The temperature should then be 28 °C for dark chocolate and 27–28 °C for white and milk chocolate. You may not need to add all the finely chopped chocolate – check the thermometer while you stir.

3. Carefully warm the chocolate up again to 31–32 °C for dark, 29–30 °C for milk and 29 °C for white chocolate. See method A point 3 for re-heating.

After tempering, chocolate can be used for coating. When you have been working with it for a while, you should warm it up again carefully to the right temperature.

Assessing and tasting chocolate

Chocolate tasting is comparable in many ways with wine tasting. The colour, flavour and aroma are assessed. In this section you will learn some of the basic points for being able to assess the quality of a chocolate.

Colour
A dark chocolate made with forastero beans will be very dark, almost black. If there are criollo beans in the chocolate, the colour will be light to reddish brown. Trinitario is a mixture of these two. Chocolate should have a smooth, shiny surface. If it is not smooth and shiny, there are two possible causes:

From the chocolate exhibition at the Bølgen og Moi restaurant, Høvikodde. © Knut Bry/tinagent

If it is whitish but smooth, it has been standing in too warm a place. Some of the cocoa butter has probably melted and been drawn up to the surface, where it has set again.

If the chocolate is whitish and rough, it has been standing in too cold a place. This causes condensation on the chocolate and the moisture on the surface melts the sugar. When the water vaporises, the sugar crystallises, forming a thin layer of sugar crystals on the outside of the chocolate.

Aroma

The scent of a dark chocolate should have a fruity undertone. Like wine, chocolate has many different bouquets. The following are some of the scents that can be recognised in chocolate:

Cherries, raspberries, blackcurrants, dates, figs, tobacco, almonds, oranges, vanilla, cinnamon, anise, toast and coffee.

NB! Chocolate should not smell burnt. If it does, it means that the beans have been roasted at too high a temperature. This is sometimes done in order to conceal the fact that the beans are of poor quality.

Flavour

To taste chocolate, break off a small piece the size of a coffee bean and put it in your mouth. Press it up against your palate with your tongue and leave it there. You must not move it.

You will soon feel the chocolate beginning to melt. Cocoa butter melts at just above 34 °C, slightly lower than the temperature inside your mouth. This makes the chocolate melt fully. A chocolate containing other hardened vegetable fats will not melt so easily, quite simply because much of the vegetable fat melts at 40 °C, and will make the inside of your mouth feel greasy.

When the chocolate melts in your mouth, it should feel smooth and even. You should not be able to distinguish particles in chocolate. If you can, it is the result of badly milled beans.

When the chocolate begins to melt, you will notice hints of different flavours.

First you taste the sweetness. You sense this with the front of the tongue. Chocolate contains little natural sugar, only about 1%, so what we taste is added sugar. If there is too much sugar, the sweet taste dominates, whereas if there is too little, the natural flavours of the chocolate are not brought out very well. Some dark chocolate contains as much as 60% sugar, while others contain as little as 20%. If you taste a chocolate with less than 30% sugar, it is often very strong and does not taste good.

After the sweetness, you taste the acid. You sense this with the sides of the tongue. Really good chocolate typically tastes of fruit acids. Chocolate with a high criollo bean content has a pronounced acidity reminiscent of red berries. Valrhona's Manjari is an example of this type of chocolate.

After registering the fruit acid taste, you notice the bitterness. Chocolate is quite bitter, but in a good chocolate, the bitterness should be present without being too predominant.

After this you taste the salts. Cocoa beans contain about 2.6% mineral salts, which you sense with the middle of the tongue. These help to intensify and combine the other flavours.

Flavours that can be tasted in chocolate: Raspberries, cherries, citrus, truffle, hazelnuts, prunes, honey, nutmeg, blackcurrants, dates, figs, almonds, vanilla, cinnamon, anise, toast and coffee.

In lower quality chocolate you can taste tannic acid, which makes the mouth feel dry, and if it is really bad it makes your tongue curl up, rather like when you chew grape pips. This is a sign that the chocolate has not been sufficiently conched (see page 11).

Some chocolate has a distinctly burnt taste. This results from some of the beans being roasted too intensely. This happens with poor consignments, where the beans that are roasted are of different sizes. If the beans are of poor quality, intensive roasting can also be a way of concealing the fact that there is not much flavour in the beans. This burnt taste does not occur in good chocolate.

A good chocolate should have a rich taste and the flavour should spread through the whole mouth. With a good chocolate, the flavour should linger in the mouth for several minutes after the chocolate has melted and been swallowed.

A brief summary

Good signs:

- The chocolate melts well in the mouth
- Does not taste very sweet
- Tastes strong and rich in the mouth
- Has a lot of fruit flavour

Bad signs:

- The chocolate does not melt well in the mouth (due to very high sugar content and/or the addition of a different fat)
- High sugar content that makes the sweet taste predominate
- Tastes bland in the mouth
- Distinct burnt flavour
- Strong taste of tannic acid
- The mouth feels greasy (due to the addition of other vegetable fats with higher melting point than cocoa butter)
- The chocolate taste quickly disappears

Valrhona chocolate

For my own recipes I prefer to use the French brand of chocolate, Valrhona. The Valrhona chocolate factory is situated in the Rhône valley, in Tain l'Hermitage, near Lyons, to be more precise. Valrhona makes what can undoubtedly be called the Rolls Royce of chocolate. Even before the beans are harvested, Valrhona is involved in deciding and picking out the cocoa beans that will go into their production, thereby assuring the quality of the product from the cocoa fruit to the finished product. Throughout the whole process, as described on page 10, they do their utmost to obtain the optimum result, as can clearly be perceived in the taste and consistency.

These are some of their kinds of chocolate, also check out all the varieties on the Web.

Guanaja 70% has a intense and powerful chocolate flavour. Its acidity, sweetness and bitterness are finely balanced, making it extremely good with citrus fruits.

Pur Caribe 66% is a fresh, fruity chocolate with a strong, dark aftertaste.

Manjari 64% has a striking fruity flavour and is made only from criolla beans, making it highly aromatic.

Caraque 56% is ideal for dipping sweets and making chocolate decorations. The combination of raw materials makes it perfect for tempering, see page 14. The good but not over-dominant chocolate flavour means that, when it is used to coat confectionery etc, it does not take too much attention away from the filling.

Jiavara 40% is a milk chocolate with undertones of caramel. It has a high percentage of cocoa for a milk chocolate, higher in fact than many Norwegian dark chocolates.

Ivoire is the French for 'ivory', and is the name of Valrhona's white chocolate. It is low in sugar but high in cocoa butter, which makes it melt well.

Melting chocolate

Never allow chocolate to come into direct with the heat source. Melt it in a bain-marie (or a microwave, see below). Use a saucepan and a stainless steel, or heatproof glass/ceramic bowl that can hang from the pan's rim without the base touching the water. Fill the saucepan with 3 cm water, put it on the hob and heat the water to boiling point. The water must not be allowed to boil but should be kept at simmering point.

Chop the chocolate finely and put it in the bowl. Place the bowl in the saucepan and stir regularly until the chocolate has melted. This will give you more control over the melting and prevent the chocolate from getting too hot. Take care that steam or other moisture does not come into contact with the chocolate.

Dark chocolate should be heated to 48–58 °C, milk and white chocolate to 45–50 °C.

Chocolate with a high cocoa mass content, i.e. one that contains a lot of cocoa butter, should be heated to a higher temperature than those with a lower cocoa mass content.

Milk and white chocolate contain dried milk, which in turn contains casein, a substance found in cheese, so the chocolate must not get hotter than 54 °C.

Chocolate can be melted in the microwave at half power. Finely chop the chocolate and melt it in short bursts of 20–30 seconds. Stir the chocolate between each burst.

Storing chocolate

Real chocolate contains vitamin E, which is a natural antioxidant and helps the chocolate keep for a long time without going rancid. However, it is important to wrap the chocolate when storing it. Chocolate easily absorbs tastes and smells and is also affected by light, so it is important to use airtight, non-transparent packaging.

Chocolate should not be kept cold. Chocolate that has been cooled is spoiled by moisture forming on it. This causes 'sugar bloom', which means that the water dissolves some of the sugar on the surface of the chocolate. Then, when the water evaporates, the sugar re-crystallises, forming larger crystals that make the chocolate gritty. You should therefore store chocolate in a dry, dark place at a temperature of between 15 and 20 °C.

Whipping cream

I always use whipping cream with a 38% fat content. When whipping cream, it is important not to beat it too long. If you do, the air is beaten out of the cream – it goes almost like curd cheese – and is too difficult to fold into consistencies like chocolate mousse. This point is often reached a little sooner than you expect. As a guide it is ready when it reaches 'soft peaks'.

It is also important that the cream should be cold when it is to be whipped, preferably as cold as 2 °C. It is a good idea to put both the cream and the equipment to be used for beating it in the freezer for a short time before whipping, unless you have an efficient electric beater.

If you are whipping cream for piping and decoration, however, it must also be stiff enough to hold its shape. To achieve this, you whip the cream a little more than to 'soft peaks'. Use your judgement.

Wine and chocolate

Chocolate is not the enemy of wine as some people claim. This is simply a huge misunderstanding. Wine and chocolate can complement each other very successfully, but certain precautions need to be taken:

- It is no use trying to rival the taste of the chocolate. The wine must match and complement the chocolate, not compete with it.

- Dessert wine must be sweeter than the dessert itself. If not, it may taste dry and sour, which is not ideal in a dessert context.
- If you want to serve red dessert wines, take care that they do not contain too much tannic acid. Unfortunately, sweet and bitter flavours in the dessert will emphasise the bitter substances in the wine. For example, a small amount of bitter cocoa will bring out the bitterness in the wine, resulting in a bitterness you really don't want with a dessert. Ingredients that can mask bitter substances include fatty constituents like cream, sweet and sour fruit and berry sauces.
- Chocolate desserts tend to be quite heavy, and you need to try and balance them. The sweeter the wine, the heavier the dessert may appear.
- It is a good idea to consider what aromas in the wine's own bouquet will match the ingredients in the dessert.

My favourites

Banyuls and Mas Amiel are sweet, red fortified wines from the south of France. Both are perfect suited to substantial chocolate desserts with a strong cocoa flavour.

I am very fond of port, but you must be careful with it, as a strong-flavoured chocolate dessert can easily bring the bitter substances in the wine to the fore too much. The more cream, butter and fruit in the dessert, the more likely it is to go with port.

Madeira and sweet sherry can safely be drunk with chocolate, as they are not at all bitter. I find these wines go extremely well with nuts and chocolate.

The history of chocolate

As far as we know, the Mayas were the first people to drink cocoa. They lived in Central America, in the areas between what is now southern Mexico and the Pacific coast of Guatemala. Cocoa beans were much sought-after in this society, partly because the people believed that cocoa had healing powers. It was also used in connection with religious ceremonies, and they made a drink they called xocoatl. The Mayas made cocoa by roasting the beans in earthenware pots and crushing them with stones. They mixed the powder they obtained with water and spices such as vanilla and chilli and sweetened it with honey.

Around AD 900, the Mayan people suddenly and inexplicably disappeared from the areas where they had lived, and after a time the Toltecs settled in the abandoned Mayan towns. Their chief god was Quetzalcoatl, who was one of a number of gods in ancient Central American mythology. Quetzalcoatl means 'the plumed serpent'. He was the god of knowledge, culture and the winds and was also called 'the lord of cocoa'. According to legend, he had originally been a much-loved and respected Toltec king. He had great knowledge of medicine, astrology and agriculture, which he shared with his people, and had collected cocoa plants on his travels. It was he who taught the Toltecs to cultivate and prepare cocoa. It was seen as a divine drink that gave people health and strength.

The king was greatly loved by his own people, but many also envied him. A wicked sorcerer put an end to the reign of the respected king by tricking him into drinking a poisonous drink that turned him mad. He relinquished his kingdom and travelled to the eastern coast, where he found a raft of snakes. He sailed away on it and was transformed into a plumed serpent, but before he left, he had promised that he would return one day and re-conquer his kingdom. This would happen in a year with the sign of the reed and he would bring with him all the riches and treasure in the world.

The Aztecs, a warlike, nomadic people, gradually overcame the Toltecs but they also prized chocolate, just as the Mayas and the Toltecs had done, and they adopted the cult of Quetzacoatl. They founded the city of Tenochtitian, now Mexico City, but the climate there was too dry for growing cocoa, so they had to have cocoa brought from far away by bearers. Each bearer carried 30 kilos, which means about 24,000 cocoa beans. Because of the transport difficulties, cocoa was a scarce commodity and was valued as highly as gold. Drinking cocoa was the preserve of the aristocracy and warriors, as the Aztecs believed it was so powerful that it was not safe to give to ordinary people. Cocoa beans were collected like treasure. They were used as payment and sacrificed to the gods. People were also sacrificed in the hope of obtaining a good crop of cocoa. In fact, cocoa beans were so valuable that the Aztec emperor Montezuma, a great consumer of cocoa, filled his treasure chamber with beans instead of gold and precious stones.

The year 1519 is said to have been under the sign of the reed, and this was the year when the Spanish conquistador Hernán Cortés arrived at the coast with a fleet of eleven ships. It is said that, when Montezuma heard about the approaching ships and the men on board wearing plumed helmets and armour that shone like snakeskin, he believed it was 'the lord of cocoa', 'the plumed serpent' or king Quetzalcoatl finally returning. The Aztecs received the Spaniards as though they were kings, and it is supposedly because of the god Quetzalcoatl that Hernán Cortés had so little difficulty in conquering the Aztec empire.

Chocolate comes to Europe

Guanaja, 1502, is a place and year that should be familiar to chocolate lovers, because it was here that Columbus anchored and tasted cocoa for the first time. He brought a sack of cocoa beans home with him and presented them to the king of Spain, but without recipes or instructions for use, they did not catch on. The sack of beans was soon forgotten. In 1528, Hernán Cortés again brought cocoa beans to

Figure of a dragon in chocolate, Nordic Confectionery Competition

Spain, this time with instructions on how they should be used. Cocoa found favour with the royal family, but it was missionaries and Spaniards who had been in the new colonies and adopted the cocoa habit who were subsequently responsible for the spread of cocoa among the clergy and aristocracy of Europe. Cocoa became a welcome means of helping monks, nuns and priests to get through Lent.

In 1585, the first trading ship carrying cocoa beans arrived in Spain. Twenty years later, Antonio Carletti, a Florentine merchant, was served chocolate while on a business trip to Spain. The taste was to his liking, and he decided to take it with him to Italy. It immediately became popular and chocolate houses or 'ciocolaterie' opened in Venice, Florence, Perugia and Turin. But the drink was still the prerogative of the aristocracy and clergy. Anne of Austria, the daughter of Phillip III of Spain, is said to have been very fond of chocolate and when she married Louis XIII of France in 1615 she took chocolate with her as well as servants who could prepare the drink. That is how chocolate came to France.

The earliest chocolate factories in Europe first appeared around 1650. They outclassed the monasteries and nunneries when it came to producing chocolate. At first the beans were ground by hand as the Amerindians did, but as industrial development progressed, new mechanical aids replaced manual work. Manufacturing is still centred around the production of drinking chocolate.

Another year worth remembering for chocolate-lovers is 1674. That was when the first slabs of chocolate came onto the market. Until that time, chocolate had only been drunk, but eating chocolate immediately became popular. In the years that followed, eating chocolate became available throughout Europe in the form of bars, slabs and pastilles.

In the 18th century chocolate appeared in art. Many artists were preoccupied by chocolate's reputation as an aphrodisiac. Erotic paintings appeared of women in negligées sitting on beds in their boudoirs drinking their morning chocolate, looking languid and alluring. In literature, it is the Marquis de Sade who is best known for spreading the fame of chocolate as an aphrodisiac. He maintained he was himself a devotee of chocolate. Europeans also credited chocolate with healing powers, and in the 18th century you could be prescribed chocolate for colds, pneumonia, diarrhoea, dysentery and cholera.

Chocolate continued its triumphal march across Europe in both solid and liquid forms, and in 1834 the first cargo of cocoa beans arrived in Norway. At first cocoa in Norway was used mainly by pharmacists, who made chocolate coatings for bitter pills, but here too it found favour with the upper classes, who were very keen to adopt continental customs. In 1852, the apothecary Carl Krafft started Norway's first chocolate factory.

As the range of machinery in Europe became more advanced, new opportunities for chocolate production gradually arose. In 1875, the Swiss Daniel Peter, made the first milk chocolate by adding dried milk, which was also a new invention. In 1879, another Swiss by the name of Rudolphe Lindt discovered that it is possible to turn rough, grainy chocolate into a smooth, shiny chocolate mass by pushing it back and forth in a container. This is the process we now call 'conching', which is an extremely important stage in the production of chocolate. So from 1879 onwards they had all the knowledge needed to produce chocolate as we know it today.

Soufflés, tarts and

other baked goodies

Chocolate Soufflé

Soufflés are a classic French dessert. 'Soufflé' means 'airy' or 'puffed up', and that is the essence of this dessert. It should rise well above the edge of the dish and be soft and airy, with a crisp crust. A soufflé is a very superior dessert that waits for no man; it must be served immediately it comes out of the oven, otherwise it collapses. The French have a saying: the soufflé does not wait for the guest, it is the guest who must wait for the soufflé.

■ ■ ■

Serves 6

6 small straight-sided china soufflé dishes, ramekins, or coffee cups that can hold about 200 ml. They must be oven-proof.

320 g dark chocolate with 66% cocoa
    mass, e.g. Valrhona Pure Caribe,
    see page 12–14
300 ml milk
30 g cornflour
4 egg yolks (80 g)
5–6 egg whites (200 g)
90 g caster

Raspberry sauce
1 vanilla pod
50 ml water
80 g caster sugar
200 g raspberries, frozen and defrosted
juice of half a lemon

Preheat the oven to 180 °C. Grease the dishes with butter warmed to room temperature. It is important to brush the butter over the vertical sides of the dishes. Sprinkle the insides of the dishes with caster sugar, tap out the excess, and set aside.

Finely chop the chocolate. Mix the milk and cornflour in a small saucepan. Bring to the boil, whisking all the time. Boil until the mixture thickens.

Remove the pan from the heat, add the chocolate and stir in thoroughly. Add the egg yolks and stir in with a whisk. Keep the mixture lukewarm.

Beat the egg whites and sugar to a meringue consistency. Add one third of the meringue mixture to the chocolate and stir in with a whisk to give a smooth mixture. Fold in the remaining meringue mixture with a spatula.

Pour the soufflé mixture into the dishes. They should be completely filled, but it is important that no mixture touches the rim, as it can burn on and prevent the soufflé from rising. Place the dishes in the oven and cook for about 10 minutes.

Serve immediately with a hot berry sauce, such as this raspberry sauce, or vanilla ice cream.

Split the vanilla pod open and scrape out the seeds. Bring the water, sugar, vanilla pod and vanilla seeds to the boil. Allow the syrup to cool.

Remove the vanilla pod. Put the syrup, raspberries and lemon juice into a food processor and blend to a smooth sauce. Strain the sauce to remove the raspberry pips.

The sauce will keep for 1 week in the refrigerator.

Chocolate loaf

A moist chocolate base filled with nuts and glazed with strong, dark chocolate icing.

In the 18th century, doctors considered chocolate to be a miracle cure. Since then much research has been done into the health benefits of eating this dark delight. Personally I am convinced that chocolate helps to cure many things. Here, for example, is a cake that will banish melancholy!

■ ■

1 loaf tin, about 1.5 litres capacity

90 g unsalted butter
85 g sugar
70 g marzipan with 50% almond
    content
2 eggs (100 g)
75 ml whole milk
20 g unsweetened cocoa powder
90 g flour
2 g baking powder
40 g chopped dark chocolate
20 g hazelnuts, roughly chopped
20 g almonds, roughly chopped
20 g pistachio nuts
20 g dried apricots, roughly chopped

Line the loaf tin with baking parchment. Preheat the oven to 175 °C.

Melt the butter in a saucepan until finger warm. Beat the sugar, marzipan and eggs in a foodmixer until frothy. Add the milk and mix in.

Pour one third of the egg mixture into the butter and whisk together. Fold this back into the remaining two thirds of the egg mixture and mix in with a plastic spatula.

Sieve the cocoa, flour and baking powder together and mix with the roughly chopped chocolate, nuts and apricots. Fold into the mixture with a spatula.

Pour the mixture into the loaf tin, which should be about two thirds full. Bake the cake for 50–60 minutes. If necessary, cover the cake with aluminium foil for the last 20 minutes of baking time to avoid it getting too dark. Remove the cake from the oven and leave for a few minutes before turning out onto a wire rack to cool completely.

Cut the chocolate loaf in slices and serve as it is, or with orange or apricot preserve and a cup of hot chocolate.

The cake can be kept for up to 2 days at room temperature. Wrap it up well in cling film when it has completely cooled. When well wrapped up, it can be kept for up to a month in the freezer.

PS! This cake is very good with a cup of hot spiced chocolate (see p. 52) on a cold winter day.

I often ice the cake with a dark chocolate icing before serving, see page 44.

Spicy slices

Chocolate in combination with different spices produces exciting flavours, and this cake is one example. Here I have added cinnamon, ginger and aniseed to the chocolate cake, and also included hazelnuts. I usually use an oven tray (a shallow, 'tray bake' tin) for this recipe. The cake can then be cut into small pieces and served as petits fours with coffee, or it can be cut into big slices for hungry people!

■

150 g hazelnuts
150 + 100 g dark chocolate with
   60–70% cocoa mass, see p. 12
250 g butter, at room temperature
200 g caster sugar
7 eggs (350 g)
120 g flour
10 g powdered cinnamon
10 g ground ginger
3 g ground anise
15 g unsweetened cocoa powder

> If you are icing the cake with dark chocolate icing, you can make patterns in it by pouring a little white icing over it. The white icing is made in the same way as the dark, but using white instead of dark chocolate. Reduce the recipe to make only 100 g white icing, if all you need is a small amount for decoration.

Line an oven tray or shallow baking tin about 40 x 25 cm with baking parchment. Preheat the oven to 180 °C.

Spread the hazelnuts on a baking sheet and roast in the oven until golden. This takes about 5 minutes, but keep an eye on them. Allow to cool before chopping roughly and tipping into a bowl.

Roughly chop 150 g dark chocolate and put in a bowl.

Finely chop 100 g dark chocolate and melt in a bain-marie or a microwave, see p. 19.

Put the butter and sugar in a foodmixer and beat until light and frothy. Scrape the mixture from the sides regularly. When the butter is light and frothy, mix in the eggs. Add the melted chocolate and mix well. The mixture will look as though it is separating, but will come together when the dry ingredients are added.

Sift the flour, spices and cocoa together and mix into the roughly chopped chocolate and the hazelnuts. Fold into the egg and chocolate mixture. It only needs to be lightly mixed together. If you mix it for too long it will become thick and sticky.

Pour the mixture into the baking tin or oven tray and bake at 180 °C for about 30 minutes. Leave the cake to cool in the tin.

When the cake is cold, turn it out and cut in pieces. Sprinkle the pieces with icing sugar or ice with dark chocolate icing, see p. 44. Ice the cake after you have turned it out but before cutting it up.

Chocolate cannelés

This is a classic small French cake, originally made without chocolate. However, chocolate, vanilla and rum combined in a soft, moist consistency and swathed in a crisp caramelised crust burst on the taste buds like a firecracker. Believe me, biting into a cannelé is extremely enjoyable.

It is important that the mixture rises sufficiently before baking. It can well be made the previous day.

These cakes are made in a special fluted mould that holds about 40 ml. The moulds should be made of metal, preferably copper, because it is such a good conductor of heat. If they are baked correctly, they should be almost crisp on the outside and soft inside.

■

Makes about 30

60 g dark chocolate with 70% cocoa
    mass, see pp. 12–14
1 vanilla pod
500 ml whole milk
50 g butter, at room temperature, +
    extra for greasing
1 egg (50 g)
3 egg yolks (50 g)
225 g icing sugar
100 g flour
5 tbsp rum (40 g)

Finely chop the chocolate and tip into a bowl. Split open the vanilla pod and scrape out the seeds.

Bring the milk to the boil with the vanilla pod and seeds. Remove the pod and gradually pour the milk over the chocolate, while stirring with a whisk. Mix together well. Add the butter in small pieces and stir it in.

Beat the egg and egg yolks lightly together with the icing sugar. Whisk the flour into the egg and sugar mixture. Then fold the chocolate mixture into the egg and sugar. Lastly, stir in the rum.

Leave the mixture to rise for 12 hours. It can be kept for 3–4 days in the refrigerator.

Preheat the oven to 200 °C. Grease the moulds with butter and fill with the mixture to about 5 mm below the edge. Bake the cannelés for about 50 minutes. Take them out of the moulds as soon as they have finished baking and leave to cool on a wire rack. If they are left in the moulds after being taken out of the oven, the outsides lose their crispness.

Eat the cakes as they are or as an accompaniment to chocolate ices or with chocolate cream.

Rum banana with chocolate sauce

This is a more exotic version of everyone's favourite banana split, for which I have marinated the banana in rum and added star anise and vanilla. It is terrific with ice cream and chocolate sauce on top.

■

Serves 4

150 g caster sugar
300 ml water
1 vanilla pod
3 star anise
juice of 1 lemon
4 tbsp brown rum
4 bananas (ripe, but firm))

Chocolate sauce
100 g chocolate with 66% cocoa
    mass content, see pp. 12–14
100 ml whole milk
25 g caster sugar

Put the sugar in a wide saucepan and heat it, stirring all the time, until it becomes a light brown caramel. Remove the pan from the heat and cautiously add the water. Be careful, it is likely to bubble and spit.

Split the vanilla pod lengthways and scrape out the seeds. Add the vanilla pod, seeds and the star anise to the saucepan, cover, and leave over low heat until the sugar grains have completely dissolved. It must not boil.

Remove the pan from the heat when the sugar is dissolved and mix in the lemon juice. Then add the rum.

Peel the bananas and slice them or cut them in half lengthways. Cover the bottom of the pan with banana (just a single layer) and cover them with syrup. Put the lid on the pan, and leave the syrup to cool at room temperature with the bananas in it.

Serve the bananas with vanilla or chocolate ice cream, see p. 67, lightly whipped cream and chocolate sauce.

Finely chop the chocolate and put in a bowl. Bring the milk and sugar to a boil. Remove the pan from the heat. Gradually pour the milk over the chocolate, stirring with a spatula. Serve the sauce lukewarm.

Savarins with chocolate cream

Savarins start out as dry cakes made of yeast dough and are then marinated in spiced syrup or rum to make them soft and juicy. They have an amusing history. When King Stanislaw I of Poland went into exile in Lorraine in 1725 and tasted the traditional local cake 'kougelopf', he thought it was quite nice but a bit dry. So to make it slide down more easily, he poured rum over it. The king was so delighted with the result that he called it after his favourite tale from the Arabian Nights, Ali Baba. That is how the cake got the name 'rum baba'. Later on, changes and improvements were made to the recipe and it was renamed after the famous French gastronome and food writer, Brillat-Savarin.

■ ■

About 25 small savarin moulds

250 ml whole milk
30 g fresh yeast
60 g caster sugar
500 g sifted flour
1/2 tsp salt
5 eggs (250 g)
150 g unsalted butter, cubed, at room
　　temperature
1 egg for brushing

Heat the milk to 30 °C. Stir the yeast into the milk. Mix the sugar, flour and salt in a foodmixer. Add the milk and stir it all together.

Add the eggs one at a time and stir well into the dough. Continue working the dough until it becomes sticky. This takes about 5 minutes at half speed. Add the butter and work it into the dough.

Cover the dough and leave to rise until it doubles in size. Knead the dough again in the foodmixer. Using two spoons, half-fill the greased moulds with the dough and set aside to rise.

Preheat the oven to 180 °C. When the dough has risen to twice the size, bake the cakes until golden. This takes about 30 minutes. Remove the savarins from the moulds and leave to cool on a wire rack.

Spiced syrup
1 vanilla pod
1 star anise
1 cinnamon stick
40 g caster sugar
1 litre orange juice
50 ml citrus liqueur, of your choice

Split the vanilla pod lengthways and scrape out the seeds. Put the pod, seeds, star anise, cinnamon stick, sugar and juice in a saucepan and bring to the boil. Set the syrup aside to cool. Add the liqueur.

Place the savarins in the cold syrup. Leave to soak for a few minutes on each side, then place on a wire rack to drip.

Chocolate cream

150 g dark chocolate with 64% cocoa
    mass, see pp.12–14

500 ml whipping cream (38% fat)

40 g glucose

20 g caster sugar

Finely chop the chocolate. Bring the cream, glucose and sugar to the boil and pour half over the chocolate so that it melts. Mix thoroughly with a spatula. Add the remaining cream and stir in. Place in the refrigerator until cold, or overnight.

Whip the cream until stiff and spoon it into a piping bag with a star-shaped nozzle. Pipe a little chocolate cream onto each savarin.

If you have any savarins left over, they can be frozen before they are soaked in the syrup.
They can be kept for about 1 month in the freezer.

Chocolate éclairs

Éclairs are classic French pastries that you can find nowadays in most cake shops. Vanilla cream was used in the original version, but here you have a recipe for éclairs filled with thick, velvety chocolate cream. These little pastries are a delight to bite into, as the choux pastry offers just enough resistance while the chocolate cream melts on the tongue. The dark chocolate icing on the top frames it all with a stronger, more distinct chocolate taste.

■ ■

Makes about 10

Choux pastry
This is a special kind of dough, as it must be first boiled and then baked. Choux pastry puffs up a lot during baking, thus creating a natural space for the filling inside.

If there is any dough left over, it can be kept for 2 days in the refrigerator or up to 2 weeks in the freezer. Frozen dough must be completely defrosted before use.

125 ml water
60 g unsalted butter
¼ tsp salt
80 g flour
2 eggs (100 g)

Chocolate cream, see p. 61, but leave out the Calvados

Dark chocolate icing, see p. 44

In a saucepan, bring the water, salt and butter to the boil. When it boils, remove the pan from the heat, cover, and set aside until the butter has melted.

Put the pan back on the heat and bring the liquid back to the boil. Add the flour and stir the contents of the pan with a wooden spoon until all the flour has been mixed into the liquid. Continue stirring until the dough comes together without sticking to the sides of the pan, about 1 minute.

Remove the pan from the heat and allow the dough to cool for 2 minutes. Mix in the eggs one at a time with an electric hand-held whisk or in a foodmixer. It is important to stir thoroughly between each egg. When the dough is ready for use it should be smooth and elastic.

Preheat the oven to 180 °C. Spoon the choux dough into a piping bag with a round nozzle of 2 cm diameter. Pipe bars of dough about 12 cm long onto a baking tray lined with baking parchment.

Bake the éclairs for about 20 minutes. It is important not to open the oven during the first half, as the éclairs may collapse. The éclairs are ready when they sound hollow when you tap them. Leave to cool on a wire rack.

Spoon the chocolate cream into a piping bag with a round nozzle. Slit the éclairs along the long side without cutting right through, like a hot-dog roll. Pipe chocolate cream into the éclairs. Dip the tops of the éclairs in chocolate icing or sprinkle them with icing sugar.

Brownies

Softening people up with chocolate is not usually very difficult, but it is always rather pleasant. Sometimes there is an added benefit, as I discovered when I got my hands on this recipe. I was actually on holiday with my wife, staying with her American relatives in Berkeley, and we were about to celebrate Thanksgiving. This harvest thanksgiving is an important festival in the States, and in keeping with tradition, all the family had gathered together for dinner. I was sitting next to tiny, sour, 90-year-old Aunt Jessie. She was not very amusing company at table, but when we came to dessert and she bit into my chocolate dish, it put her in a better mood. It turned out that Aunt Jessie had a weakness for dark chocolate. After a long chat about chocolate and all its positive attributes, I was given her special brownie recipe – and it is good!

■

1 oven tray or shallow baking tin, 40 x 25 cm

Preheat the oven to 150 °C and line the oven tray with baking parchment.

200 g dark chocolate with 64% cocoa mass, e.g. Valrhona's Manjari, see pp.12–14
200 g butter

Finely chop the chocolate and melt in a bain-marie together with the butter. Make sure all the chocolate has melted.

4 eggs (200 g)
340 g caster sugar
240 g flour
1 tsp baking powder
125 g pecan nuts, roughly chopped

Add the eggs and mix thoroughly with a whisk. Add the sugar and beat in well. Sift together the flour and baking powder, add the pecan nuts and stir into the chocolate mixture.

Spoon the mixture into the oven tray and smooth it out. Bake for about 40 minutes. Allow to cool in the tray at room temperature. Cut in pieces and sprinkle with icing sugar before serving.

Brownies may be kept in the refrigerator for up to 4 days, or up to 2 weeks in the freezer if well wrapped in clingfilm.

Always serve brownies at room temperature.

Chocolate cream timbales

This dessert is always welcome. Chocolate cream never goes out of fashion. I usually mix in a little citrus liqueur; dark chocolate counterbalances the acids in the citrus very well and I think it gives the cream a slightly more unusual and interesting flavour.

■ ■

For this I use small aluminium moulds holding 100 ml.

Serves 10

150 g dark chocolate with 64% cocoa
    mass content, see pp. 12–14
6 gelatine leaves
300 ml whipping cream (38% fat)
300 ml whole milk
40 g caster sugar
2 egg yolks
4 tbsp citrus liqueur, of your choice

Set the oven to 160 °C. Place a bain-marie in the oven. There should be enough water in the container so that it is almost at the same height as the mixture in the moulds.

Finely chop the chocolate and tip into a bowl. Soak the gelatine in cold water for at least 5 minutes. Pour the cream and milk into a saucepan and bring to the boil.

Whisk the sugar, eggs and egg yolks together lightly in a bowl. Gradually add the hot milk to the egg mixture while stirring with a whisk. Squeeze the water out of the gelatine leaves and melt them completely in the hot liquid. Mix well. Pour about one third of the hot liquid over the chocolate and stir with a spatula in the middle of the chocolate until you have a smooth, shiny mixture.

Gradually add the remaining liquid, stirring constantly. The mixture should be smooth and even. If desired use an electric hand-held mixer. Add liqueur to taste. Pour the hot mixture into the moulds.

Put the moulds in the bain-marie in the oven. The water should be hot enough to be steaming. Leave the dessert in the oven for about 20 minutes. If the mixture has cooled down a lot before it is put in the oven, it will take longer. If the creams begin to rise, the oven is too hot. Move the moulds a little to check if the creams have set – they should be firm in the middle.

Remove the moulds from the oven and leave to cool in the re-frigerator for at least 3 hours. Insert a small knife down around the edges of the timbales to let air in between the cream and the mould. Turn the timbales out onto a plate. Serve with chocolate sauce, see page 32, or with fresh berries.

Criollo tart with raspberries

For this tart I have used chocolate made from the most exclusive and aromatic cocoa beans there are, namely criollo beans. The chocolate is called Manjari and is made by Valrhona. This chocolate is characterised by a strong berry flavour, which is enhanced when served with red berries such as raspberries and really comes into its own. Use it if at all possible.

■ ■

Serves 8

One tart tin, 22 cm diameter.

For the base
200 g cold unsalted butter in 2 cm cubes
100 g icing sugar
300 g flour
1 egg

> If there is pastry left over from the tart base, it can be wrapped in clingfilm and kept in the freezer for up to 3 weeks.

Filling
150 g dark chocolate with 64% cocoa
   mass, e.g. Valrhona's Manjari, see
   pp.12–14
3 gelatine leaves
1 vanilla pod
300 ml whipping cream (38% fat)
15 ml raspberry liqueur (20 g)

Rub the butter and sugar into the flour in a bowl by hand or in a foodmixer.

Add the egg and knead into the dough by hand or quickly mix the dough in the foodmixer.

Wrap the dough in clingfilm and set aside to rest for at least 4 hours in the refrigerator. It can be left overnight. Roll out the dough to a thickness of 3 mm and lay it in a greased tart tin. Prick the base with a fork. Put it in the freezer for 30 minutes to allow the dough to harden.

Preheat the oven to 180 °C. Take the tart base out of the freezer, cover it with baking parchment and fill with dried peas or lentils. This is called 'baking blind' and prevents the base from rising and the sides from sinking during baking.

Bake the tart base in the centre of the oven for 8 minutes. Remove the baking parchment and peas and bake the base for about another 5 minutes until golden brown. Leave to cool.

Finely chop the chocolate and melt in a bain-marie to about 50 °C. Soak the gelatine leaves in cold water for about 5 minutes. Split open the vanilla pod and scrape out the seeds.

Bring the cream, vanilla pod and vanilla seeds to the boil. Remove the pan from the heat and remove the vanilla pod. Squeeze the water out of the gelatine leaves and melt them completely in the hot cream. Pour the cream onto the chocolate in a thin stream, stirring in small circles with a spatula to form a smooth emulsion with the chocolate and the cream. It is important not to use a whisk, because it would

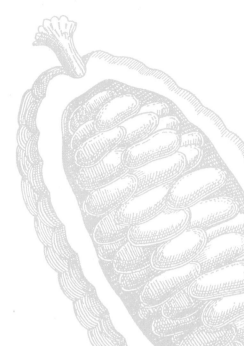

cause air bubbles in the filling. If you use a plastic spatula or a wooden spoon, you will get a smooth, shiny filling. Add raspberry liqueur to taste.

Pour the filling into the baked tart base and put it to cool in the refrigerator until the filling has set firm. This takes about 4 hours. Decorate the tart with fresh raspberries before serving.

Tips

The chocolate tart should stand at room temperature for about 15 minutes before serving to bring out the flavour.

When cutting up the tart, it is best to use a knife that has been warmed, for example by dipping it in hot water and drying it. Then the knife melts its way through the chocolate filling and makes a neater cut.

Dark chocolate icing

200 g dark chocolate with 50%
    cocoa mass, see pp.12–14
120 ml whipping cream (38% fat)
50 g caster sugar

Finely chop the chocolate and melt in a bain-marie, see p.19.

Bring the cream and sugar to the boil. Pour the cream onto the chocolate in a thin stream, stirring in small circles with a spatula to make an emulsion with the chocolate and the cream. It is important not to use a whisk, because it would cause air bubbles in the filling. If you use a spatula or a wooden spoon, you will get a smooth, shiny icing.

Put the cake on a wire tray and pour the icing over it, smoothing it with a metal spatula.

This icing can be kept in the freezer for up to 1 month. When you want to use it again, defrost it and warm it carefully in a bain-marie on the hob or in short bursts in the microwave.

Chocolate crêpes with soufflé

Crêpes are thin pancakes that are generally available in both sweet and savoury versions. This version is sweet and has chocolate added to it. But what makes it really special is that it is filled with soufflé, and being cooked in both the pan and the oven gives it a crisp consistency. It is, quite simply, a rich, extremely tempting chocolate pancake.

■ ■

Serves 5: about 10 pancakes

120 g flour
2 tbsp unsweetened cocoa powder
20 g caster sugar
3 pinches salt
2 eggs (100 g)
300 ml whole milk
20 g butter
60 g dark chocolate with 70% cocoa
   mass, see pp. 12–14
Sunflower or soya oil for greasing
   the pan

Mix the flour, cocoa, sugar, salt, eggs and milk in a bowl to make a smooth batter.

Melt the butter. Finely chop the chocolate, melt it in the warm butter and then blend it into the mixture. Leave the batter to stand and rise for 60 minutes.

Warm the frying pan until you can feel the heat when you hold your hand over it. Brush the pan with a pad made from kitchen paper and dipped in oil.

For a 22-cm (8½-in.) frying pan I use about 40 ml batter per pancake. Take care to spread the batter out in a thin layer before it sets firm. Fry the pancake on both sides.

Stack the pancakes one on top of the other and cover with a cloth to keep in the heat.

Soufflé mixture

1 half or whole vanilla pod, depending
   on your taste
100 ml + 50 ml whole milk
40 g caster sugar
12 g cornflour
2 egg yolks (40 g)
20 g butter
50 g caster sugar
4 egg whites (120 g)

Preheat the oven to 180 °C

Split the vanilla pod lengthways and scrape out the seeds.
Put 100 ml milk, the vanilla pod, seeds and the 40 g sugar in a small saucepan (the saucepan should not be more than half full), stir together and heat to boiling point.

Put the remaining milk and the cornflour in a bowl and whisk lightly together, then beat the egg yolks into the milk and cornflour mixture.

Gradually pour two thirds of the vanilla flavoured milk into the egg mixture, stirring with a whisk.

Then pour the custard sauce mixture back into the saucepan. Bring the custard sauce to the boil and simmer for 1 minute, stirring the bottom of the pan continuously with the whisk (use a sturdy hand whisk), so that it does not catch. Remove the vanilla pod after the sauce has thickened. Stir the butter into the hot sauce and pour into a bowl.

Beat together the 50 g sugar and the egg whites to make a meringue. Fold half the meringue into the vanilla cream with a whisk, then fold in the remainder with a plastic spatula.

Put 2 tbsp soufflé mixture in the centre of each pancake and spread out to within 1 cm of the edge. Fold the pancakes in two and place them on a baking sheet lined with baking parchment. Bake in the oven at 180 °C until the soufflé mixture has risen and turned golden. This takes about 8 minutes.

Serve the crêpes immediately, perhaps with a citrus fruit salad, see p.118.

Drinks and soups

'Chocolate is not just nice, it is also balm for the mouth. It is useful and gives good health. That is why all those who drink cocoa have pleasant breath.'
Thus wrote Doctor S. Blancardi of Amsterdam in 1705.

The original chocolate

In the empire of the Aztec ruler Montezuma, cocoa beans were prized as much as gold. People thought that the magical power of cocoa was so strong that it would be dangerous for ordinary people to drink it, so only the warriors and other high-ranking persons were given xocoatl, or cocoa. At Montezuma's court, they drank chocolate with vanilla, chilli, honey and water added. Montezuma himself is said to have drunk 50 cups per day. In fact he kept cocoa beans in his treasure chamber instead of gold and precious stones. Here is a recipe for chilli cocoa inspired by the Aztecs.

■

Serves 2

100 g dark chocolate with 70% cocoa
    mass, e.g. Valrhona's Guanaja, see
    pp. 12–14
1 vanilla pod
400 ml water
20 g unsweetened cocoa powder
1 cm fresh chilli
70 g honey
2 tsp cornflour blended with 2 tbsp
    cold water

Finely chop the chocolate. Split the vanilla pod and scrape out the seeds. Put the vanilla pod, seeds, water, cocoa powder, chilli and honey in a saucepan and bring to the boil. Stir in the cornflour and simmer for about half a minute.

Remove the pan from the heat and gradually pour the contents over the finely chopped chocolate, while stirring with a whisk.

TIPS
Chocolate drinks taste best if allowed to stand overnight and warmed up again next day. Immediately before serving, I usually whip the chocolate briskly with a hand whisk or whisk it a little with an electric hand-held mixer to make it frothier. Pour into small cups and serve.

Spiced hot chocolate

In the 18th century chocolate was very popular as a means of increasing one's libido. One of the stories told about Madame de Pompadour, the official mistress of the 18th century king Louis XV of France, is that she drank chocolate to make her more passionate. Louis, however, accused her of being ice-cold, so either the chocolate did not work or someone else enjoyed the benefits of the aphrodisiac effects of chocolate.

The Comtesse de Barry, another prominent lady at the French court, is said to have been so passionate that it was impossible to satisfy her. To get things going, or stir things up, she served her lovers chocolate with strong, hot flavourings such as cayenne pepper and chilli. Here is a recipe for an aphrodisiac dating from that time.

■

Serves 2

1 vanilla pod
100 g dark chocolate with 70% cocoa
    mass, e.g. Valrhona's Guanaja, see
    pp. 12–14
400 ml whole milk
2 tbsp caster sugar
1 tbsp honey
2 cm fresh chilli
1 stick cinnamon

Split the vanilla pod lengthways and scrape out the seeds. Finely chop the chocolate.

Put all the ingredients except for the chocolate in a saucepan and bring slowly to the boil. Remove the pan from the heat and gradually pour the milk over the finely chopped chocolate while stirring with a whisk.

Strain the drink before pouring it into small cups and serve with lightly whipped cream.

Cold Amaretto chocolate

When chocolate came to Spain in the 16th century, it first became popular among pious men and women of the church, who drank it during Lent. But gradually, a few people began to claim that chocolate was a stimulant and there was disagreement about whether it was permissible to drink it during a fasting period. After much discussion to and fro, Pope Pius V declared in 1569: 'This drink does not break the fast', and if the Pope said so, it must be true! But when it comes to the Amaretto chocolate in this recipe, I am afraid it must be classed as a stimulant.

Serves 1

50 g dark chocolate with 56% cocoa
    mass, see pp.12–14
100 ml whole milk
1 tbsp caster sugar
3 tbsp vanilla ice cream
2 tbsp Amaretto

Finely chop the chocolate. Bring the milk and sugar to the boil and pour onto the chocolate. Mix well and leave to cool.

Run the drink through the blender with vanilla ice cream and Amaretto. Pour into glasses filled with ice cubes.

Cold mint chocolate

In the 18th century, the clergy drank chocolate to help them through the hard times of Lent. At first they mixed the chocolate with water, but then some French nuns came up with the idea of mixing it with sugar and milk instead. No doubt this invention made the Lenten fast considerably more enjoyable! Cocoa as we know it is therefore over 300 years old. Here I have added mint to the cocoa as well, a heavenly combination of flavours.

■

Serves 1

20 g dark chocolate with 56% cocoa
　　mass, see pp.12–14
2 'After Eight' mint chocolates
100 ml whole milk
2 tbsp vanilla ice cream

Finely chop the chocolate. Break the mints in pieces and add them to the chocolate.

Bring the milk to the boil and pour it over the chocolate. Stir well, and allow to cool. Put it through the blender with the vanilla ice cream. Pour into glasses filled with ice cubes.

Cold coffee chocolate

'Chocolate is the drink of the nobility. Coffee, on the other hand, is the comfort of simple folk.' So said Ludvig Holberg, the 18th-century Norwegian playwright. Here I have put the two drinks together, which I hope will provide comfort for both simple and noble folk.

■

Serves 1

50 g dark chocolate with 66% cocoa
　　mass, see pp. 12–14
100 ml whole milk
1 tbsp sugar
50 ml espresso or strong coffee
2 tbsp vanilla ice cream

Finely chop the chocolate. Bring the milk to the boil, stirring to dissolve the sugar, and pour it over the chocolate. Stir well, and allow to cool.

Put the drink through the blender with the espresso and the vanilla ice cream. Pour into glasses filled with ice cubes.

Cold rum chocolate

Belief in the positive attributes of chocolate was widespread in the 18th century. For example, a Swedish priest by the name of Father Labat claimed that 'Chocolate alone contains sufficient nourishment for a person of any age.' Personally, I am most concerned with the idea that chocolate should fulfil the need for something nice, and I think the combination of chocolate and rum in this drink does just that.

■

Serves 1

50 g dark chocolate with 66% cocoa
    mass, see pp. 12–14
100 ml whole milk
1 tbsp vanilla ice cream
2 tbsp brown rum

Finely chop the chocolate. Bring the milk to the boil and pour it over the chocolate. Stir well, and allow to cool.

Put the drink through the blender with the vanilla ice cream and rum. Pour into glasses filled with ice cubes.

Chocolate with cinnamon and Grand Marnier

Chocolate, orange and cinnamon is a delicious combination of flavours. This is a perfect drink for putting you in the Christmas spirit and preparing for festive cheer.

■

Serves 2

100 g dark chocolate with 70% cocoa
    mass, e.g. Valrhona's Guanaja,
    see pp. 12–14
400 ml whole milk
1 piece orange peel, about 4 x 4 cm,
    all pith removed
3 tbsp sugar
1 small cinnamon stick
2 tbsp Grand Marnier

Finely chop the chocolate. Bring the milk and orange peel to the boil and set the pan aside.

Melt the sugar with the cinnamon stick in a saucepan until the sugar is a light caramel. Pour the milk over the caramel. If there are pieces of caramel in the milk, leave it to stand until the caramel has completely dissolved.

Gradually pour the milk over the finely chopped chocolate, while stirring with a spatula. Add Grand Marnier to taste. Strain the cocoa and serve in small cups.

Tea and chocolate soup with floating islands

Tea and chocolate may seem a slightly unusual combination to many people, but that does not mean it is not good. The 'floating islands' are a delicious addition, giving extra body and sweetness. Tea and chocolate soup is a nice, light dessert, suitable for both summer and winter.

■ ■

Serves 8

Tea and chocolate soup

200 g dark chocolate with 64% cocoa
    mass, see pp. 12–14
1 vanilla pod
550 ml whole milk
60 g sugar
10 g Earl Grey tea

Finely chop the chocolate and tip into a bowl. Split the vanilla pod lengthways and scrape out the seeds.

Bring the milk to a boil with the sugar, vanilla pod and seeds. Remove the pan from the heat and add the tea. Allow to draw for about 4 minutes. Strain the milk and pour it over the chocolate, while stirring with a spatula.

Put the soup through a blender or use an electric hand-held mixer. Place in the refrigerator to chill.

Floating islands

For poaching the eggs:
50 ml whole milk
1 piece orange peel, about 5 x 5 cm,
    without pith
3 egg whites (100g)
50 g icing sugar
50 g glucose
20 g grated coconut

Heat the milk with the orange peel in a wide saucepan to just below boiling point. Cover and lower the heat to keep the milk at just below boiling point.

Beat the egg whites, sugar and glucose to a stiff meringue. Fold the grated coconut into the meringue. Using two tablespoons, form the meringue into egg shapes.

Put the 'eggs' into the hot milk and poach for about 3 minutes. Turn them after 1½ minutes. Remove with a slotted spoon to a plate and set aside to cool. Discard the milk.

Before serving:

1 mango

Peel and cut the mango in pieces. Carefully pour the chilled chocolate soup, into wide soup plates. Place the pieces of mango and the floating islands into the soup and serve.

The soup may be served with mango crisps:

100 g mango flesh
30 g caster sugar

Whizz the mango flesh and sugar in a blender. Place spoonfuls of purée on a baking sheet lined with baking parchment and spread them out so they are thin. Bake the crisps in the oven at 150 °C until dry. This takes about 30 minutes. Remove the crisps from the tray and leave to cool. When cold, they should be crunchy.

Coconut soup with chocolate cream

Here is an unrecognisable variation on grandmother's sago soup. Coconut milk, orange peel and ginger are the somewhat exotic ingredients. I actually got the inspiration for this soup in Singapore, because I was working for a few days at the majestic Fullerton Hotel, where I was served fascinating staff meals prepared by Singhalese and Chinese cooks.

■ ■ ■

Serves 4

Coconut soup
250 ml whole milk
125 ml whipping cream (38% fat)
1 tbsp caster sugar
1 piece orange peel, about 2 x 2 cm
    without pith
2 cm fresh ginger, peeled
30 g tapioca or sago (about 3 tbsp)
200 ml canned coconut milk

Bring all the ingredients except the coconut milk to the boil and simmer until the tapioca pearls are transparent, about 15 minutes.

Let the soup cool and stir in the coconut milk. If the soup is thick, it may be thinned with a little milk.

Chocolate cream
140 g dark chocolate with 64% cocoa
    mass, see pp. 12–14
1 vanilla pod
200 ml milk
200 ml whipping cream (38% fat)
3 egg yolks (50 g)
70 g caster sugar

Finely chop the chocolate and melt in a bain-marie, see p. 19.

Split open the vanilla pod and scrape out the seeds. Put the vanilla pod, vanilla seeds, milk and cream in a saucepan and bring to the boil. Lightly whisk the egg yolks and sugar together.

Gradually pour the hot milk over the egg mixture, while stirring with a whisk. Then strain the custard sauce back into the saucepan. Have a bowl and a strainer ready to strain the sauce.

Heat the sauce while constantly stirring with a wooden spoon to prevent the custard settling on the bottom of the pan.

When the mixture thickens (85 °C) – this happens very quickly with small quantities like these – it should be strained into a bowl.

Gradually pour the hot vanilla sauce over the chocolate, while stirring with a wooden spoon. Mix the cream with an electric hand-held mixer or in a blender. Pour into small bowls holding about 50 ml. Set aside to cool overnight. It needs a little time to itself in order to set.

Before serving:
2 passion fruit

Serve the soup with the chocolate cream. Put a spoonful of passion fruit flesh in the soup before serving. It can also be served with crispy fried pastry, see p. 173.

Apple soup with chocolate-filled brandy snaps

My wife and I were in Normandy one summer, in Caen, to be precise. We went on a French course there and at the same time we did some research on Normandy country cooking. Every Sunday there is a market in Caen. It begins in the early hours of the morning. I am not an early riser, but when it is a matter of food, I can make the effort. So we went to the market and stood breathing in the mixture of herbs, fruit, fresh pastries, chocolate, caramels and coffee. We found ourselves in front of a mountain of apples, and the man standing behind them was waving his arms and shouting and pointing to some bottles. It was apple brandy. The farm he came from was famous for its Calvados. It was with all these scents in my nostrils and a bottle of Calvados in my hand that I invented this dessert, a fresh, slightly acid apple soup with Calvados and brandy snaps filled with chocolate.

■ ■ ■

Serves 4

Chocolate cream
125 g dark chocolate with 70% cocoa
    mass, see pp. 12–14
3 egg yolks (60 g)
40 g caster sugar
40 ml + 230 ml whipping cream
    (38% fat)
4 tbsp Calvados

Finely chop the chocolate and melt in a bain marie, see p. 19.

Put the egg yolks in a bowl and add the sugar, beating gently with a whisk.

Bring 40 ml cream to the boil and pour over the eggs, beating gently.

Pour the melted chocolate into the egg mixture, while stirring with a whisk.

Whisk 230 ml cream until light and creamy, see p. 19.

Wait until the chocolate mixture is lukewarm (40 °C) before folding in the cream with a spatula. Add Calvados to taste. Pour the chocolate cream into a bowl and place in the refrigerator until it sets. This takes about 3 hours.

Apple soup
400 ml unsweetened apple juice
20 g sugar
1 tsp cornflour blended with 2 tbsp
    cold water
1 small bunch lemon balm

1 apple (Granny Smith)

Bring the apple juice and sugar to the boil. Add the blended cornflour and beat it into the soup. Bring the soup to the boil and simmer for half a minute.

Let the soup cool before putting it through the food processor with the lemon balm (both stalks and leaves), to taste. Strain the soup through a fine strainer and set aside in a cool place.

Brandy snaps

80 g butter, at room temperature
80 g caster sugar
1 tbsp glucose or light honey
4 tbsp flour

Preheat the oven to 180 °C. Mix all the ingredients together in a bowl with a hand whisk. Place teaspoons of the mixture 10 cm apart on a baking sheet lined with baking parchment. Bake the biscuits until golden, 2–3 minutes.

Remove the baking sheet from the oven and 'lift' the biscuits off the sheet round a rolling pin. Then roll the biscuits round a sharpening steel or the handle of a wooden spoon to form a tube, see p. 170. This must be done swiftly as the biscuits harden quickly and then you will have to put them back in the oven to become soft again. Make two rolls for each person.

Fill a piping bag with chocolate cream and pipe it into the brandy snaps. Pipe in cream from both ends.

Before serving:
Peel the apple. Cut into small cubes or use a melon scoop and make little balls. Add them to the soup. Ladle the soup into bowls and serve with the brandy snaps on the side.

I often serve this soup with a little cinnamon foam:

Bring 100 ml skimmed milk to the boil with 1 tsp caster sugar and half a cinnamon stick. Remove the pan from the heat and beat briskly with a hand whisk or whisk the milk with a hand-held mixer until foam forms on the top. With a spoon, place a little foam on each bowl of soup.

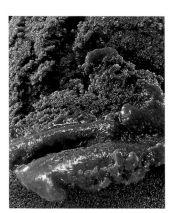

Ices and sorbets

The Chinese are said to have been the first to make ice cream. Many important personalities in world history are said to have been very fond of ice cream, for instance King Solomon, the emperor Nero, and the great doctor of ancient times, Hippocrates. The latter is said to have been interested in the healing properties of ice cream – he prescribed it as a remedy for various diseases. In addition, he believed it increased the vital juices and recommended it highly to men.

Ice is therefore not a modern phenomenon and, as far as we know, the Chinese got there first, but it was here in Europe that ice cream and chocolate met – and what a wonderful union!

Chocolate sorbet

The ice King Solomon ate was probably melted snow with fruit juice added to it and then sweetened with honey. This is similar to a kind of sorbet. The method for making sorbet has been somewhat refined over the years, and the velvety sorbet in my recipe here is the result of great progress in dessert cuisine.

■ ■

Serves 10

150 g dark chocolate with approx. 64% cocoa mass, e.g. Valrhona's Manjari, see pp. 12–14
550 ml water
100 g caster sugar
40 g glucose
1 egg white

Finely chop the chocolate and tip into a bowl.

Bring the water, 70 g of the sugar and glucose to the boil. Pour the sugar syrup over the chocolate and stir to a smooth mixture. Place the mixture in the freezer.

Stir the sorbet briskly with a whisk every 15 minutes from when it begins to freeze until it begins to go 'slushy'. This takes about 2 hours.

Whisk the egg white and the remaining sugar to a meringue and fold into the slushy sorbet. Put the sorbet back in the freezer and stir with a whisk every 15 minutes until it begins to set, about 1 hour. Leave the sorbet in the freezer for 1 hour without stirring. Take it out and serve in small chilled bowls.

If you plan to keep the sorbet in the freezer for some time, move it to the refrigerator 15 minutes before serving, so that it can soften slightly.
Bon appétit!

Chocolate ice cream

It was Marco Polo who introduced the recipe for ices made with fruit and milk to Europe. He had brought this recipe home from China. The popularity of ices among the upper classes reached new heights as a result of this innovation. The Italians, still famous for their fantastic ice cream, soon began to develop the idea and when the Florentine princess Catherine de Medici married Henri de Valois, the future Henri II of France, in 1533, one of the things she brought with her was a 'machine' for making ice cream. That was how ices made with milk came to France, and since then they have continued their triumphal march across the whole of Europe and the rest of the world. Here is a recipe for chocolate ice cream with a strong chocolate flavour.

■ ■

Serves 8

90 g dark chocolate with 64% cocoa
    mass, see pp. 12–14
400 ml whole milk
25 g glucose or light honey
100 g caster sugar

Finely chop the chocolate and tip into a bowl. Put the milk, glucose and sugar in a saucepan and bring to the boil. Gradually pour the warm milk onto the chocolate while stirring with a whisk to give a smooth and even mixture. Chill the ice cream mixture in the refrigerator before freezing it in an ice cream maker.

If you do not have an ice cream maker, you can freeze the ice cream in the freezer. Stir the ice regularly when it begins to freeze. When it gets slushy, stir it with a hand-held mixer or in a food processor. Do this every 30 minutes until the ice cream sets hard. This takes about 2 hours. Finally put it to stand in the freezer for about 40 minutes to set. If you follow this procedure the result will be quite similar to what you get using an ice cream maker.

If you plan to keep it in the freezer for some time before serving, move it to the refrigerator 15 minutes before serving, so it gets a bit softer.

Serve the ice cream in a cornet made of tuile biscuit see p. 171.

Milk chocolate ice cream à la Singapore

Milk chocolate ice cream with a lychee and raspberry salad is a wonderfully refreshing dessert. It came into existence late one evening in Singapore when I was working at the Fullerton Hotel. I was exhausted after working so hard for so many guests, but on the way out I passed a huge consignment of lychees. Lychees are sweet, juicy Chinese fruits with a delicious scent of flowers. I stood there for a while and suddenly saw before me a fantastic dessert. I got so enthusiastic that I found my second wind and started to try it out. It was early morning before I got to bed.

■■

Serves 8

145 g milk chocolate with 40% cocoa
    mass, e.g. Valrhona's Jiavara,
    see pp. 12–14
400 ml whole milk
25 g glucose or light honey
45 g caster sugar

Finely chop the chocolate and tip into a bowl. Bring the milk, glucose and sugar to the boil. Gradually pour the warm milk onto the chocolate while stirring with a wooden spoon or spatula so the chocolate melts thoroughly. It is a good idea to stir the mixture with an electric hand-held mixer afterwards. Chill the ice cream mixture in the refrigerator before freezing it in an ice cream maker.

If you do not have an ice cream maker, you can freeze the ice cream in the freezer. Stir the ice regularly till it begins to freeze. When it gets slushy, stir it with a hand-held mixer or in a food processor. Do this every 30 minutes until the ice cream sets hard. This takes about 2 hours. Finally put it to stand in the freezer for about 40 minutes to set. If you follow this procedure the result will be quite similar to what you get using an ice cream maker.

If the ice cream is to remain in the freezer for some time before being served, it should be moved to the refrigerator 15 minutes before serving, so it gets a bit softer.

Lychee and raspberry salad
1 vanilla pod
100 g fresh raspberries
100 g lychees, fresh or tinned
1 tbsp caster sugar

Split the vanilla pod lengthways and scrape out the seeds. If using fresh lychees, remove the shells and stones. Mix the vanilla seeds with the sugar and fold into the raspberries and lychees. Stand the salad in the refrigerator for 1 hour before use.

Serving:
Put a little lychee and raspberry salad in a bowl. Place a scoop of ice cream on top and serve immediately.

May be served with wafer-thin chocolate caramel as well, see p.172.

Chocolate parfait hearts

I made these chocolate parfaits for my wife on Valentine's Day, and she was absolutely delighted with them. Chocolate parfait has proved to be good for our relationship on a number of occasions, so I can warmly recommend it.

Unlike cream ices and sorbets, parfait does not need to be stirred or mixed in an ice cream maker during freezing, because the combination of raw materials in parfait prevents ice crystals from forming during freezing.

■

Serves 8

150 g milk chocolate with 40% cocoa
    mass, see pp. 12–14
1 vanilla pod
125 g crème fraîche
2 egg yolks (40 g)
20 g caster sugar
3 tbsp Amaretto (almond liqueur)
150 ml whipping cream (38% fat)

Finely chop the chocolate and melt in a bain-marie, see p. 19.

Split the vanilla pod lengthways and scrape out the seeds. Put the crème fraîche, vanilla pod and vanilla seeds in a saucepan and bring to the boil.

Beat the egg yolks and sugar together lightly. Gradually pour the hot crème fraîche over the egg mixture while stirring with a whisk. Remove the vanilla pod.

Mix the hot custard with the melted chocolate using a whisk. Start by adding one third of the custard to the chocolate and blending until the mixture is smooth and even. Then gradually add the remainder, stirring constantly.

Set the chocolate mixture aside to cool on the worktop for 5 minutes until lukewarm, about 35 °C. Add Amaretto to taste.

Whip the cream, see p. 19, and fold one third into the chocolate mixture with a spatula. Then fold in the remaining cream.

Fill the moulds with parfait – I use silicone heart-shaped moulds – or you could use muffin tins holding about 100 ml. Stand the parfaits in the freezer for at least 3 hours.

If well wrapped, parfait may be kept frozen for 14 days. Take it out of the freezer 10 minutes before serving and arrange on plates. Serve with red berries.

Chocolate parfait with citrus liqueur

Chocolate and citrus go very well together, because the citric acid is a perfect counterbalance for the acid in the chocolate and gives it a fresh, slightly tart flavour.

I made this parfait in cone-shaped moulds. Cut A4 OHP film, or acetate sheet, in half diagonally to form triangles. Make these into cones and tape together. Put them point down in a bowl of sugar to hold them steady.

■ ■

Serves 8

115 g dark chocolate with 56% cocoa
    mass, see pp. 12–14
30 g caster sugar
3 tbsp Grand Marnier (25 g)
3 egg yolks (60 g)
250 ml whipping cream (38% fat)

Finely chop the chocolate and melt in a bain-marie or a microwave, see p. 19.

Beat the sugar, Grand Marnier and egg yolks until stiff. Whip the cream, see p. 19. Fold the egg and sugar mixture into the chocolate and mix well with a hand whisk. Fold in half the cream with a plastic spatula. Finally, fold in the remaining cream.

Fill the cones or other moulds with parfait and stand in the freezer for at least 3 hours.

If well wrapped, parfait may be kept frozen for 14 days. Take it out of the freezer 10 minutes before serving and arrange on the plate.

The parfait may be served with fresh berries or an orange and passion fruit sauce.

Orange and passion fruit sauce
100 ml orange juice
100 g sugar
1 tsp cornflour blended with
1 tbsp water
1 passion fruit

Bring the orange juice and sugar to the boil. Add the cornflour mixture and stir in thoroughly with a whisk. Simmer for half a minute.

Cut the passion fruit in two, scoop out the flesh and add to the sauce. Mix everything together with an electric hand-held mixer or run it through a blender.

Set the sauce aside to cool. It will keep for 1 week in the refrigerator.

Confectionery

The first chocolate bar came onto the market in 1650, and it did not take long for creative spirits to find out how they could combine fruit, spices and liqueurs with solid chocolate in the same way as they had done with drinking chocolate. The result was confectionery.

People in Norway eat a lot of sweets and chocolate at Christmas and Easter, and are gradually beginning to do so for Valentine's Day too. The British are also keen chocolate eaters and not just on special occasions either! The French, on the other hand, do not restrict themselves to these festivals and I was amazed when I saw a 10-metre long queue outside Pierre Hermé's chocolate shop in Paris on a boiling hot Friday afternoon in August. When, hot and exhausted, I finally got inside, it was like entering another world. The sunlight was left behind outside, the interior was air-conditioned and tastefully decorated in walnut brown wood and subdued colours. The counter was groaning under the weight of confectionery, macaroons, chocolate cakes and biscuits, and I suddenly felt very much at ease and appreciated why a hot summer day was a good day for buying chocolate.

Chocolate caramels

Sweet, chewy caramels with a strong chocolate flavour can be recommended for Christmas, Easter, Valentine's Day, and actually they are good to eat at any time. Chocolate caramels put me in a very good mood, so you must not disregard the fact that they can lift the spirits a few notches. Just experiment and enjoy the results!

■ ■

Makes about 40

90 g dark chocolate with 70% cocoa
    mass, e.g. Valrhona's Guanaja,
    see pp. 12–14
210 g caster sugar
210 g glucose
30 g butter
330 ml whipping cream (38% fat)

Line an oven tray or shallow baking tin with baking parchment. Finely chop the chocolate and set aside.

Mix all the ingredients except for the chocolate in saucepan and heat to 116 °C, stirring the bottom of the pan occasionally. Add the finely chopped chocolate and mix everything together thoroughly.

Pour the mixture into the oven tray to give a layer 1 cm thick and leave to cool at room temperature. It can be cut in pieces the following day. Wrap the caramels in cellophane and keep in a dry place.

From the left: egg liqueur chocolates, citrus marzipan and Palet d'Or

Egg liqueur chocolates

Chocolates containing egg liqueur (advocaat) are extremely good, and, even better, these have been rolled in roasted coconut as well. The coconut gives it a firmer consistency and, what is more, the combination of roasted coconut and advocaat is particularly delicious.

■ ■

Makes about 80

200 g grated coconut
250 g white chocolate
60 ml whipping cream (38% fat)
10 g glucose
25 g butter, at room temperature
3 tbsp advocaat

300 g tempered dark chocolate for dipping, see p. 14

Preheat the oven to 180 °C. Toast the coconut for about 5 minutes, but keep watch, until golden brown. Allow to cool.

Finely chop the chocolate and melt in a bain-marie, see p. 19.

Bring the cream and glucose to the boil and pour it over the chocolate. Stir until the mixture is smooth. Cool the mixture to 34 °C. Stir in the butter and advocaat. Put the mixture to cool overnight at 12–16 °C. When the mixture has set, make small balls about the size of a cherry using a melon scoop or a small spoon. Dip them in tempered dark chocolate and roll them in the toasted coconut. Leave them in the coconut in a cool place (not the refrigerator) for a while so that the chocolate sets.

Citrus marzipan

Adding citrus liqueur to marzipan gives it a fantastic taste and consistency. To counterbalance the sweetness in the marzipan, I dip it in dark chocolate. This is a good Christmas sweet and is easy to make..

■ ■

Makes about 20

200 g marzipan, preferably with an almond content of 40–60%
4 tbsp Grand Marnier
Orange food colouring
300 g tempered dark chocolate for dipping, see p. 14

Mix the marzipan thoroughly with the Grand Marnier. Roll into balls weighing about 10 g. Press them gently with a finger on the top and make a little hollow with a wooden stick so they look like an orange. Brush them with food colouring.

Allow the balls to dry for a day at room temperature. Dip the bottoms in tempered dark chocolate. Stand them on baking parchment until the chocolate sets. Keep the sweets in an airtight container at room temperature.

Palet d'Or

Palet d'Or is a classic French chocolate. Both the shape and the gold leaf on the top are standard. I tasted it for the first time when I was working at the restaurant Bagatelle, and what a discovery it was!

■ ■ ■

Makes about 80

300 g dark chocolate with 66% cocoa
    mass, see pp. 12–14
200 ml whipping cream (38% fat)
20 g glucose
20 g butter, at room temperature

300 g tempered dark chocolate with
    56% cocoa mass, e.g. Valrhona's
    Caraque, see p. 14, for dipping
    a little gold leaf for decoration

See picture on p. 78

Finely chop the chocolate and tip into a bowl. Bring the cream and glucose to the boil and pour over the finely chopped chocolate. Stir until the mixture is smooth. Begin stirring in the middle of the bowl in small circles with a wooden spoon or spatula. If the mixture does not become smooth and elastic, it is a good idea to stir it briefly with an electric hand-held mixer or in a foodmixer.

Cool the mixture to 34 °C. Stir in the butter. Pour the mixture into a tray lined with baking parchment to give a layer 5 mm thick.

Stand the mixture to cool overnight at 12–16 °C. Remove the mixture from the tray and cut into 2 cm squares with a sharp knife, or cut out rounds of 3 cm diameter with a pastry cutter. Warm the knife or pastry cutter a little in hot water and dry it, so it is easier to cut out the sweets.

Dip the squares or rounds in tempered dark chocolate and stand them on OPH film, an acetate sheet, or a smooth surface such as clingfilm stretched tight over a chopping board.

Place the chocolates in the refrigerator for 1 minute. Take them out and let them stand for 60 minutes on the film. If the chocolate is well tempered, it will become very shiny on the side lying against the film surface. Turn the pieces over and decorate with a little gold leaf.

From the left: Citrus liqueur chocolates, raspberry chocolates and citrus balls with gin

Citrus liqueur chocolates

Chocolate and oranges are traditional fare for Easter ski trips in Norway. This classic French confection contains the same combination, and taking some with you when you go skiing is not such a bad idea.

■ ■ ■

Makes about 80

280 g dark chocolate with 70% cocoa
　　mass, see pp. 12–14
200 ml whipping cream (38% fat)
20 g caster sugar
20 g glucose
20 g butter, at room temperature
2 tbsp citrus liqueur, e.g. Grand Marnier
　　or Cointreau
300 g tempered dark chocolate with
　　56% cocoa mass, e.g. Valrhona's
　　Caraque, see p. 14, for dipping
Dried apricots for decoration

See picture on p. 81

Finely chop the chocolate and tip into a bowl. Bring the cream, sugar and glucose to the boil and pour over the finely chopped chocolate. Stir until the mixture is smooth. Begin stirring in the middle of the bowl in small circles with a wooden spoon or spatula. If the mixture does not become smooth and elastic, it is a good idea to stir it briefly with an electric hand-held mixer or in a foodmixer.

Cool the mixture to 34 °C. Stir in the butter and liqueur. Pour the mixture into a tray lined with baking parchment to give a layer 5 mm thick.

Stand the mixture to cool overnight at 12–16 °C. Remove the mixture from the tray and cut into 2 cm squares with a sharp knife. Warm the knife a little in hot water and dry it, so it is easier to cut out the sweets.

Dip the squares in tempered dark chocolate and stand them on a sheet of baking parchment. Decorate with a piece of apricot. Place the chocolates in the refrigerator for 1 minute. Then take them out and let them stand at room temperature.

Raspberry chocolates

Raspberries, chocolate and hazelnuts are a good combination. The lightly acid taste of the raspberries brings out the fruitiness in the chocolate, and the hazelnuts both enhance the flavours and add body to the chocolates. The result is a deliciously fresh confection.

■ ■

Makes about 80

200 g chopped hazelnuts
300 g milk chocolate with 40% cocoa
 mass, see pp. 12–14
200 g frozen raspberries, defrosted
5 g glucose
10 g unsalted butter, at room temperature

300 g tempered dark chocolate with
 56% cocoa mass for dipping,
 see p. 14

See picture on p. 81

Preheat the oven to 180 °C. Roast the hazelnuts for about 10 minutes until golden brown. Allow to cool.

Finely chop the chocolate. Whizz the raspberries in a blender and sieve out the pips. Measure the quantity. You need 100 ml raspberry purée.

Bring the raspberry purée and glucose to the boil together and pour over the finely chopped milk chocolate. Stir until the mixture is smooth. Begin stirring in the middle of the bowl in small circles with a spatula. If it does not all melt, place the bowl in a bain-marie and warm gently while stirring constantly, or mix it briefly to a smooth mixture with an electric hand-held mixer or in a foodmixer. Cool the mixture to 34 °C. Stir in the butter until smooth.

Stand the mixture to cool overnight at 12–16 °C. When the mixture has set, make balls the size of cherries using a melon scoop or a small spoon. Dip them in tempered dark chocolate and roll them in the chopped hazelnuts. Let them stand in the hazelnuts for a while for the chocolate to set.

Citrus balls with gin

Gin and lemon are two flavours that work very well together, and combined with chocolate they make a fresh, slightly tart confection.

■ ■

Makes about 60

300 g milk chocolate with 40% cocoa
    mass, see pp. 12–14
25 ml whipping cream (38% fat)
50 ml freshly squeezed lemon juice
5 g glucose
10 g butter, at room temperature
1 tbsp gin

300 g tempered milk chocolate for di-
    pping, see p. 14
200 g icing sugar for decoration

See picture on p. 81

Finely chop the chocolate and tip into a bowl. Bring the cream, lemon juice and glucose to the boil and pour over the chopped chocolate. Begin stirring in the middle of the bowl, making small circles with a wooden spoon or spatula. Stir until the mixture is smooth. If the mixture does not become smooth and elastic, stir it briefly to a smooth mixture with an electric hand-held mixer or in a foodmixer.

Cool the mixture to 34 °C. Stir in the butter and gin. Stand the mixture to cool overnight at 12–16 °C. When the mixture has set, make balls the size of cherries using a melon scoop or a small spoon.

Dip the sweets in tempered dark chocolate and roll them in the icing sugar. Let them stand in the sugar for a while for the chocolate to set.

Whisky sticks

I made these chocolates after visiting to my brother in Edinburgh. He took me on a whisky tasting trip to the Scottish Highlands. I brought a lot of samples of excellent Scotch whisky home with me, and a large number of them ended up in a batch of confectionery.

Makes about 80

240 g dark chocolate with 70% cocoa
    mass, see pp. 12–14
125 ml whipping cream (38% fat)
20 g glucose
25 g caster sugar
60 g butter, at room temperature
4 tbsp whisky (25 g)

approx. 200 g dark chocolate for dipp-
    ing
approx. 150 g icing sugar for decoration

See picture on p. 86

Finely chop the chocolate and tip into a bowl. Bring the cream, glucose and sugar to the boil and pour over the finely chopped chocolate. Stir until the mixture is smooth. Begin stirring in the middle of the bowl in small circles with a wooden spoon or spatula. If the mixture does not become smooth and elastic, it can be a good idea to stir it briefly to a smooth mixture with an eletric hand-held mixer or in a foodmixer.

Stir in the butter and add whisky to taste. Cool the mixture until it thickens and spoon it into a piping bag with 1-cm smooth nozzle. Pipe the mixture into sticks on a board covered with baking parchment. Stand to cool overnight in a cool place (12–16 °C).

Cut the sticks into pieces 4 cm long. Dip them in melted chocolate and roll them in icing sugar. The chocolate does not have to be tempered. I usually take a little chocolate in my hands, then pick up a few sticks and cover them with a thin layer of chocolate. It is good to have two people working on this job, so the other one can cover them with icing sugar. Leave the sweets lying in the icing sugar for while for the chocolate to set.

Instead of whisky, these sweets can be made with other types of spirit such as Calvados or rum. They can also be rolled in cocoa instead of icing sugar.

Candied orange peel with ginger

Orange, ginger and vanilla are strong tastes that work well together and enhance each other. In combination with dark chocolate they cause a sizzling explosion of flavour. It is important to use dark chocolate with a high cocoa mass content to allow the chocolate to counterbalance the acid in the candied oranges.

■ ■ ■

Makes about 120

10 oranges

1 vanilla pod
1 litre water
juice of 1 lemon
3 cm fresh ginger
1 tbsp glucose
400 + 400 + 400 + 400 + 400 g sugar
300 g dark chocolate with 56% cocoa
    mass, e.g. Valrhona's Guanaja, see
    pp. 12–14

Divide the oranges into six segments, leaving the peel on. Cut out the flesh and eat it or make freshly squeezed juice. Put the peel in a pan, cover with cold water and bring to the boil. When it boils, strain off the peel. Put the peel back in the pan and fill up again with cold water. Bring to the boil and strain. The peel should be boiled up five times.

Split the vanilla pod lengthways and scrape out the seeds. Put the pod and seeds in the pan with the orange peel. Add 1 litre water, the lemon juice, ginger, glucose and 400 g sugar. Bring to the boil, cover and simmer for about ½ hour. Add another 400 g sugar, cover and continue simmering for about ½ hour. Repeat until all the sugar has been added and the peel has boiled for 2½ hours. Leave the lid off the last two times. Leave the pan and its contents to cool overnight.

Remove the orange peel and all the pith and cut lengthways in strips 5 mm thick. Lay them on a tea towel to drain and dry them well.

Temper the dark chocolate, see p. 14.

Dip the strips of orange peel in the tempered chocolate and lay them on baking parchment until the chocolate sets. Keep in an airtight container at room temperature.

Whisky sticks, recipe p.85, and
candied orange peel with ginger

Caramelised almonds

Caramelised almonds make me think of old Christmas stories and windows with red checked curtains. They are nice, simple Christmas goodies.

■ ■

100 g almonds
30 g sugar
100 ml water
1 tsp butter

If desired, 300 g dark chocolate

Put all the ingredients except the butter in a wide pan. It is important that there should not be more than two layers of almonds in the pan, otherwise it may be difficult to achieve a good result.

Put the pan over high heat and boil until almost all the water has evaporated, stirring at regular intervals. When the water begins to evaporate, the sugar will collect as a white coating around the almonds. At this point it is important to stir the almonds the whole time. The sugar will gradually turn to caramel and form a thin skin around the almonds.

Remove the pan from the heat, add the butter and stir in thoroughly. Tip the almonds onto a sheet of baking parchment. Pull them apart while still warm so they do not set in clusters. Let the almonds cool and keep in airtight packaging at room temperature.

Eat the almonds as they are or cover with dark chocolate.

Temper 300 g dark chocolate, see p. 14. Stir the cooled almonds into the chocolate. Pour the chocolate and almond mixture onto a sheet of baking parchment and smooth it over. Allow the mixture to cool, then break in pieces for serving.

Stuffed dates

Dates stuffed with marzipan are delicious, and here I have added pistachio nuts, dried apricots and honey as well. The crowning glory is rolling the dates in cocoa, making them the de luxe version of Christmas goodies. PS! They are extremely good with a little mulled wine.

■ ■

Makes about 30

100 g blanched almonds
300 ml water

75 g icing sugar
1 vanilla pod
1 tsp honey
20 g pistachio nuts, roughly chopped
50 g dried apricots, roughly chopped

30 dates
approx. 100 g icing sugar for decoration
approx. 100 g unsweetened cocoa
    powder for decoration
100 g dark chocolate for dipping

If the almonds have not been blanched, put the almonds in a heat-proof bowl. Bring the water to the boil and pour over them. Leave the almonds to stand in the water for about half an hour. Strain off the water and remove the skins.

Note! If you are using almonds that have already been blanched, they still need to stand in the water for half an hour. It is important that they absorb moisture.

Put the almonds in a food processor with the icing sugar. Split the vanilla pod lengthways, scrape out the seeds and add them to the almond mixture. Reserve the pod for later use. Add the honey. Blend the mixture until it is smooth and has the consistency of coarse marzipan.

Scoop the mixture out onto the work surface. Knead in the pistachios and apricots by hand. Form the mixture into balls the size of cherries.

Cut open the dates and remove the stones. Fill the dates with the almond balls and roll them in your hands to the shape of a rugby ball.

Mix the icing sugar and cocoa powder together. Melt the chocolate, see p. 19. The chocolate does not need to be tempered.

Dip the dates in the melted chocolate and roll them in the mixture of icing sugar and cocoa. I usually take a little chocolate in my hands, pick up a few dates and cover them with a thin layer of chocolate. It is good to have two people working on this job, so the other one can cover them with the icing sugar and cocoa mixture. Leave the dates lying in the icing sugar for a while for the chocolate to set.

Chocolate palettes with nuts and apricots

These are pretty little artists' palettes, and even though I say it myself, they do taste as good as they look. Hazelnuts, pistachios and dried apricots are excellent with chocolate. They give it flavour and body, so you really can sit there munching and enjoying the taste.

■ ■

Makes about 50

500 g milk chocolate with 40% cocoa mass, e.g. Valrhona's Guanaja, see pp. 12–14
200 g assorted dried fruits and nuts, cut in pieces, e.g. hazelnuts, apricots, pistachios, almonds

Finely chop the chocolate, melt and temper it, see p. 14. Spoon the chocolate into a piping bag with a 5 mm smooth nozzle and pipe rounds about the size of a 50-pence coin. Leave them to stand for a few minutes so they begin to set. They must not set completely.

Decorate the tops with chopped nuts and apricots. Stand them to cool at 12–16 °C.

You could also use white and dark chocolate to make the palettes.

Biscuits

Almond macaroons

If you want to experience a very special confectionery and patisserie, I recommend Ladurée in Paris. As you enter the venerable mint-green shop you feel as if you have stepped back in time to the Romantic period. The first room is quite dark but your eyes are drawn immediately to a massive counter made of dark wood. Lying on it are macaroons, neatly arranged in groups according to size and colour – mint green, lilac, pink, yellow, brown, and so on. Then you go further into the café, and there are round tables with lace tablecloths, impressively draped white lace curtains, with ornaments and pictures hanging from the ceiling and on the walls. When you bite into, for instance, my favourite – a sweet, crisp, pink macaroon filled with thick, slightly tart raspberry cream – you are lost to this world.

Macaroons are my absolute favourites when it comes to cakes and biscuits. They are a brilliant invention with a crisp surface and a soft, chewy centre. You can eat them as they are or use them as an accompaniment to things like ices and parfaits.

■ ■

Makes about 60

130 g blanched almonds
170 g icing sugar
3 egg whites (100 g)
80 g caster sugar
Yellow food colouring (optional)
Anise seeds for garnishing

Finely grind the almonds with the icing sugar in a food processor and pass through a sieve.

Whip the egg whites and caster sugar to a stiff meringue.

Fold the ground almonds into the meringue with a spatula. Do not work too hard, or the mixture will not hold together well. If desired, add a few drops of yellow colouring.

Use a piping bag to pipe rounds 2 cm in diameter onto a baking sheet lined with baking parchment. Sprinkle with a few anise seeds.

Set the oven to 170 °C. Leave the macaroons to stand on the worktop and dry out for 20 minutes. They should be dry on top before you bake them for 15–20 minutes.

Wait for the macaroons to cool before removing them from the baking parchment. They should be soft inside and crisp outside. If they are too crisp, put them in the refrigerator overnight.

Put the macaroons together in pairs with a little chocolate and passion fruit cream in between.

Chocolate and passion fruit cream

100 g milk chocolate with 40% cocoa mass, see pp. 12–14

3 passion fruits

25 ml whipping cream (38% fat)

1 tsp butter

Finely chop the chocolate and melt in a bain-marie or a microwave, see p. 19.

Cut open the passion fruit and scrape out the contents. Mix the passion fruit with the cream and blend in a food processor. Strain out the seeds. Press the seeds against the strainer with a tablespoon to make sure you get all the liquid out.

Bring the liquid to the boil and pour it over the melted chocolate, stirring with a whisk. Add the butter and stir in. Beat the mixture well with the whisk so it becomes thick and shiny.

Chocolate sablé (shortbread)

I got this recipe from the mother of a French friend from Brittany. This shortbread did not originally have chocolate in it, but I think a little dark, bitter chocolate spices it up.

■

Makes about 30

50 g dark chocolate with 70% cocoa
    mass, e.g. Valrhona's Guanaja,
    see pp. 12–14
140 g butter
4 egg yolks (80 g)
140 g caster sugar
200 g flour
12 g baking powder

Roughly chop the chocolate. Melt the butter and cool to finger warm.

Beat the egg yolks and sugar until stiff, add the cooled butter and stir in with a spatula.

Mix the flour, baking powder and chocolate together and fold into the egg mixture. Stand the mixture in the refrigerator until it begins to solidify. This takes about 1½ hours.

Preheat the oven to 160 °C. Roll the mixture out to a thickness of about 5 mm. Cut out rounds about 4 cm in diameter with a biscuit cutter.

Arrange the rounds on a baking sheet lined with baking parchment, leaving about 5 cm between the rounds, as they will expand a little. Bake for about 20 minutes until golden. Leave to cool on a wire rack.

The biscuits can be kept in an airtight container at room temperature for about 1 week.

> I usually bake the rounds in the rings I use to cut them out with. That way they are perfect spheres, but you do need to have lots of cutters to do this!

Cookies

These biscuits have a nice rounded chocolate taste and a crisp consistency. The addition of the pieces of chocolate, hazelnuts and dried apricots gives them that little bit extra in terms of taste and texture.

■

300 g butter
250 g caster sugar
200 g demerara
450 g flour
2 eggs (100 g)
150 g dark chocolate, roughly chopped
100 g hazelnuts, roughly chopped
100 g dried apricots, chopped
1/2 tsp salt of hartshorn (ammonium carbonate)
1/2 tsp baking powder
1 tsp ground cinnamon
1 tsp unsweetened cocoa powder

Mix the butter, sugar and demerara sugar in a foodmixer for 1 minute at half speed. Add flour and egg alternately and mix into the dough. Then add the remaining ingredients and mix everything together thoroughly.

Roll the dough into sausage shapes 4 cm in diameter. Place in the freezer to harden. This takes about 20 minutes.

Preheat the oven to 180 °C. Take the rolls of dough out of the freezer and cut them in rounds 1.5 cm thick while still hard. Lay the rounds on a baking sheet lined with baking parchment and bake for about 20 minutes until they begin to brown. Leave to cool on a wire tray. Keep the biscuits in an airtight container at room temperature.

Frozen rolls of dough may be kept for up to 1 month in the freezer if well wrapped in cling film.

Hazelnut sticks

Hazelnuts and chocolate are a frequently used combination of taste and texture. These hazelnut sticks are crisp and really delicious to munch on. I have dipped them in dark chocolate, which results in a terrific snack that can be enjoyed on its own or used as an accompaniment to ices, mousses and creams.

■ ■

400 g hazelnuts
300 g caster sugar
15 g cornflour
7 egg whites (200 ml)

300 g dark chocolate, 60–70%
    cocoa mass

Preheat the oven to 180 °C. Spread the hazelnuts on a baking sheet and bake in the oven until they begin to brown. This takes about 5 minutes. Allow the nuts to cool.

Put all the ingredients except for the egg whites in a food processor and grind until the hazelnuts are finely chopped. Pour the mixture into a saucepan and add the egg whites. Heat the mixture, stirring constantly with a spatula. It is important to scrape the mixture from the bottom of the pan all the time. When the mixture begins to warm it will thicken and the egg whites will gradually turn whitish. The mixture should begin to steam, but not boil.

Remove the pan from the heat and allow the mixture to become lukewarm. Spoon it into a piping bag with a nozzle with a 1 cm opening. Pipe long sticks onto a baking sheet lined with baking parchment. The mixture is quite hard, so it may be a good idea to use a strong piping bag. If desired, the dough may be rolled into balls with the diameter of a 20-pence coin.

Bake the sticks for about 15 minutes until golden. Remove from the oven and cut them in shorter 4-cm lengths while they are still warm. Set aside to cool.

Dip the finished sticks in tempered dark chocolate, see p. 14.

Keep the sticks in an airtight container at room temperature.

Spiral tea biscuits

These are classic tea biscuits, decorative and very tasty. Vanilla and chocolate are a match made in heaven and the almonds provide an extra edge.

PS! These biscuits are easier to make than they look.

■

Pale dough

50 g blanched almonds
1 vanilla pod
100 g icing sugar
250 g flour
150 g butter, straight from the re-
    frigerator, cubed
1 egg (50 g)

Finely chop the almonds in a food processor. Split the vanilla pod lengthways and scrape out the seeds. Reserve the pod for future use.

Blend the vanilla seeds, icing sugar, flour and butter together with the almonds in the food processor. Process until the butter has crumbled together with the dry ingredients. Add the egg and blend in. Remove the dough and press it out to a 4-cm thick square. Wrap the dough in clingfilm and place in the refrigerator for at least 1 hour, or overnight.

Chocolate dough

30 g blanched almonds
250 g flour
25 g cocoa powder (4 tbsp)
100 g icing sugar
150 g butter
1 egg (50 g)
1 egg white, for brushing

Follow the same procedure as for the pale dough, but add the cocoa powder at the same time as the flour.

Roll the pale dough out so it is about twice as long as it is wide, and about 5 mm thick.

Do the same with the chocolate dough. Brush off the flour used for rolling. Brush the pale dough with a little water and lay the chocolate dough on top. Roll together lightly. Then roll up the dough together into a sausage shape from the long side. Place the roll in the refrigerator to harden, about 20 minutes.

Preheat the oven to 180 °C. Cut the roll in slices about 1 cm thick. Arrange the slices on a baking sheet lined with baking parchment and brush them with white of egg. Bake for about 20 minutes until golden.

Biscotti

Biscotti are an Italian classic. Italians generally have a great deal to be proud of when it comes to making sweet things. If you are someone who likes to crunch your way through almonds and hazelnuts in delicious combination with dark chocolate, then this biscotti recipe is made for you.

■ ■

120 g blanched almonds
100 g hazelnuts
150 g butter
230 g caster sugar
380 g flour
1½ tsp baking powder
Grated rind of 1 orange
3 eggs (150 g)
1 egg white, for brushing

Dark chocolate for dipping, if desired

Preheat the oven to 180 °C. Spread the almonds and hazelnuts on a baking sheet and bake in the oven until golden. This takes about 15 minutes. Allow the nuts to cool.

Mix the butter, sugar, flour, baking powder and orange peel in a foodmixer. Add the eggs and mix in. Then mix in the cooled nuts.

Roll the dough into long sausages shapes 3 cm in diameter. If the dough is soft, put it in the refrigerator for a few minutes to harden. Place the rolls in the refrigerator for about 1 hour.

Preheat the oven to 180 °C. Put the rolls on a baking sheet lined with baking parchment. There should be about 10 cm between the rolls, as they will rise and expand. Brush the rolls with white of egg. Bake for about 40 minutes until golden.

Remove the rolls from the oven (leave the oven on) and cut in slices about 5 mm thick with a sharp bread knife. It is important to use a sawing action to avoid the nuts just getting pressed through the slices. This must be done while the rolls are warm or it will not work. Put the slices back, flat, on the baking parchment, and bake for a further 10 minutes. Allow to cool.

When the biscotti have cooled, they may be dipped in tempered dark chocolate, see p. 14. Only dip half the biscuit in the chocolate.

Keep the biscuits in an airtight container at room temperature.

Chocolate diamonds

These biscuits may not be as imposing as the name might suggest, but chocolate diamonds are very good and go perfectly with a cup of tea or coffee. Some Italian friends of mine usually make them for Christmas and serve them with orange or apricot preserve. I find them delicious all the year round.

■

Makes about 80

300 g unsalted butter, at room
    temperature
100 g butter, at room temperature
160 g icing sugar
2 egg yolks (40 g)
40 g unsweetened cocoa powder
450 g flour
1 egg, for brushing
200 g granulated sugar for decoration

Cream together the butters and sugar in a foodmixer. This can also be done with a hand-held electric mixer or even manually. Take care that the butters are soft before you start. Beat until creamy, but the mixture should not go frothy. Scrape the mixture down from the sides of the bowl at regular intervals.

Add the egg yolks and mix together thoroughly. The mixture will look as if it has separated, but it will come together when the dry ingredients are added. Sift together the cocoa powder and flour and blend into the mixture. Note! It must only be blended lightly. If you stir too much after adding the flour, the dough will become elastic.

Roll the dough into long 3-cm thick sausages shapes. Wrap in clingfilm and place in the refrigerator until they harden. This takes about 2 hours. At this point the rolls may be frozen and kept for about 1 month in the freezer before they have to be baked.

Preheat the oven to 180 °C. When the rolls of dough are hard, take them out and remove the clingfilm. Brush the rolls with lightly beaten egg and roll them in sugar. Cut in slices about 1.5 cm thick. Arrange the slices on a baking sheet lined with baking parchment, about 3 cm apart. Bake in the centre of the oven for about 15 minutes. Allow the biscuits to cool on a wire rack.

The biscuits can be kept for about 1 week in an airtight container at room temperature.

Viennese shortcake with cocoa

This is a classic Austrian biscuit shaped like a W, after the venerable old Wittamer cake shop in Vienna where it originated. The biscuit is sweet, rich and crisp and almost melts in the mouth. There is no cocoa in the classic recipe, but in my experience the round, mild biscuit tastes perfect with chocolate.

■

150 g butter, at room temperature
100 g icing sugar
1 egg (50 g)
260 g flour
25 g unsweetened cocoa powder
(4 tbsp)

Preheat the oven to 180 °C. Cream together the butter and icing sugar in a foodmixer or an electric hand-held whisk. This can also be done by hand. Take care that the butter is soft before you start. Beat the egg into the butter. The mixture will look as if it has separated, but it will come together when the dry ingredients are added. Sift together the cocoa and flour and blend into the mixture. It must be blended lightly. If you stir too much after adding the flour, the dough will become elastic.

Spoon the mixture into a piping bag with a star-shaped nozzle and an opening of about 1.5 cm. The mixture is so firm that it may be worth only putting in one third of the mixture at a time.
Pipe small wave or W shapes onto a baking sheet lined with baking parchment. Pipe them so that the W is pressed together. The size of the biscuits should be about 5 x 3 cm.

Bake the biscuits in the centre of the oven for about 10 minutes. Allow to cool on a wire rack. These biscuits are perfect with a cup of tea or as an accompaniment to ice cream.

The biscuits can be kept for about 1 week in an airtight container at room temperature.

Mousses, bavaroises and creams

El Grande

This gateau was created for my friend and brother-in-law, the composer Jono el Grande. I would like to claim that a fancy cake has a lot in common with a piece of music. Just as in a musical composition, all the elements must contribute to the creation of perfect harmony. And what is it that makes a gateau special? I think the secret is finding a perfect balance between sweetness, richness, tartness and texture. This one has a hazelnut base that is both crisp and chewy, on top of which is a layer of rich, almond and hazelnut cream. These are classic components in the world of patisserie, but in this recipe an added piquancy comes in the form of a slightly tart lemon cream. This counterbalances the sweetness to perfection. And so that it can truly live up to its splendidly grandiose name, it is coated in dark chocolate icing.

■ ■ ■ ■

Hazelnut base
1 baking sheet, 30 x 25 cm

90 g hazelnuts
30 g flour
100 g icing sugar
5 egg whites (150 g)
50 g caster sugar

Preheat the oven to 180 °C. In a food processor, grind the nuts with the flour to give a fine meal. Mix the nut flour with the icing sugar.

Beat the egg whites and sugar to a stiff meringue. Fold the nut mixture into the meringue with a spatula.

Line a baking sheet with baking parchment and spread the mixture out in a 1.5-cm thick layer. Bake the base in the centre of the oven for about 20 minutes. Try lifting a corner of the base. If it comes away from the baking parchment, the base is ready. Set aside.

Chocolate wrapper
1 baking sheet, 30 x 25 cm

6 egg yolks (120 g)
100 g + 100 g caster sugar
6 egg whites (180 g)
50 g unsweetened cocoa powder

Preheat the oven to 180 °C. Beat the egg yolks and 100 g sugar to a frothy mixture.

Beat the egg whites and the second 100 g sugar to a stiff meringue. Combine the meringue and the egg yolk mixture using a spatula. Sift the cocoa into the mixture and fold it in gently.

Cover a baking sheet with baking parchment. Spread the mixture over the baking parchment with a spatula in a 1-cm thick layer.

Bake in the centre of the oven for about 20 minutes. When the base comes away easily from the baking parchment, it is ready. Turn the base upside down onto a fresh sheet of baking parchment sprinkled with sugar and remove the paper it was baked on. Set aside.

Lemon cream

125 ml freshly squeezed lemon juice
100 g caster sugar
1 large egg (70 g)
4 egg yolks (80 g)
10 g cornflour
80 g cold unsalted butter, cubed

Whisk all the ingredients except for the butter together in a sauce-pan. Bring the mixture to the boil, whisking continuously.
Let the mixture simmer for about 20 seconds, stirring the bottom of the pan with the whisk so that it does not catch.

Pour the mixture into a bowl. Stir the butter into the hot lemon cream with a hand whisk. It is important to stir the butter in as it melts.

Make tubes of OHP film or an acetate sheet with a diameter of 1–1.5 cm and fill with the lemon cream. Place in the freezer. Once frozen, remove the OHP film and wrap them in the chocolate base. Set aside again in the freezer.

Almond and hazelnut cream

80 g caster sugar
60 g almonds
60 g hazelnuts
50 ml water

3 gelatine leaves
125 ml whipping cream (38% fat)
125 ml whole milk
25 g caster sugar
3 small egg yolks (50 g)
225 ml whipping cream (38% fat)

In a saucepan, mix 80 g sugar with the almonds, hazelnuts and water, heat and allow to boil. When the water has evaporated and the sugar has turned white, stir the mixture until the sugar has carameli-sed.

Pour the mixture onto a sheet of baking parchment and allow to cool a little. When the sugar has set but is still warm, tip the mixture into a food processor. Process it for as long as the nuts go on releas-ing oil and the mixture becomes fluid and smooth. This takes about 10 minutes.

Soak the gelatine leaves in cold water.

Bring the 125 ml cream and the milk to the boil. Beat the egg yolks and sugar together lightly in a heatproof bowl. Gradually pour the hot liquid into the egg mixture, while stirring with a whisk.

Find a bowl and a strainer. Pour the custard sauce back into the pan and heat, while stirring the bottom of the pan with a wooden spoon. It is important to stir continuously to avoid the egg yolk setting at the bottom of the pan.

When the mixture has thickened (85 °C), it should be strained into the bowl. Squeeze the water out of the gelatine leaves and add them to the hot sauce. Stir well so the gelatine dissolves completely into the sauce.

Blend the sauce with the nut mixture. Put the sauce to cool in the refrigerator or in a bain-marie with cold water and ice cubes. It is important to stir the sauce at regular intervals (every 5 minutes) until it reaches room temperature so that it sets evenly.

Whisk the 225 g cream and fold into the sauce when the sauce has cooled to room temperature.

Assembling:
Line a 1.2 litre 'roof-gutter' mould with baking parchment.

Fill the mould with almond and hazelnut cream to 2 cm below the edge. Lay the frozen chocolate-wrapped lemon cream on it and press down into the nut cream.

Cut the hazelnut base to size and lay it on the top

Put the mould in the freezer overnight, or until frozen right through. This takes 6 hours.

To serving:
Remove from the mould. The baking parchment will ensure it comes away easily. Then place on a wire rack and cover with the dark chocolate icing. Leave the cake to defrost in the refrigerator for about 3 hours.

Dark chocolate icing
200 g dark chocolate with 60% cocoa
    mass, see pp. 12–14
50 g caster sugar
25 g glucose or light honey
200 ml whipping cream (38% fat)

Finely chop the chocolate and melt in a bain-marie, see p. 19. Bring the sugar, glucose and cream to the boil. Pour the cream onto the chocolate in a thin stream, stirring in small circles with a spatula to make an emulsion with the chocolate and the cream. Don't use a whisk or you will create air bubbles in the filling. If you use a spatula or a wooden spoon you will get a smooth, shiny icing.

Chocolate cream with citrus fruit salad

Orange and pineapple make a sharp, tangy and tasty combination and go perfectly with rich vanilla and chocolate cream. Here is a lovely fresh dessert that is equally suitable for summer or winter.

This cream is first prepared as a vanilla cream. Finely chopped chocolate is then added after it is finished. When making vanilla cream make sure you boil for 1 minute. The starch in the cornflour must have time to gelatinise, so that the cream will retain its moisture. If it does not gelatinise, the vanilla cream will soon begin to release liquid and become watery.

■ ■

Serves 10

60 g dark chocolate with 64% cocoa
    mass, see pp. 12–14
1 vanilla pod
200 ml + 50 ml whole milk
75 ml whipping cream (38% fat)
55 g caster sugar
20 g cornflour
2 egg yolks (30 g)

Finely chop the chocolate and tip into a bowl. Split the vanilla pod lengthways and scrape out the seeds.

Put the 200 ml milk, the vanilla pod and seeds, cream and sugar in a saucepan (the pan should not be more than half full), stir together and bring to the boil.

Pour the 50 ml milk and the cornflour into an heatproof bowl and whisk lightly together. Beat in the egg yolks.

Gradually pour two thirds of the hot mixture into the egg mixture, stirring with a whisk.

Then pour this mixture back into the saucepan. Bring to the boil and simmer for 1 minute, stirring the bottom of the pan constantly with a whisk (use a sturdy hand whisk) so that the cream does not catch.

Remove the vanilla pod when the cream has boiled. Add the chocolate and stir into the hot cream with a whisk until smooth.

Pour the cream into individual bowls, cover with clingfilm and set aside to cool.

Citrus fruit salad

4 oranges

200 ml orange juice

1 pineapple

1 vanilla pod

100 g sugar

Peel the oranges, remove the pith and skin from the segments of flesh and set aside. Squeeze the juice from any remaining pieces of the orange and mix with the 200 ml orange juice.

Peel the pineapple and cut in half lengthways. Remove the core and discard. Cut the pineapple flesh in chunks 2 x 2 cm.

Split the vanilla pod lengthways and scrape out the seeds. Put the vanilla pod and seeds, sugar, orange juice and pineapple chunks in a saucepan and bring to the boil. Cover and simmer for about 10 minutes. Set aside to cool. When it has cooled, add the segments of orange.

May be served with chocolate caramel, see p. 170.

The chocolate cream can be kept in the refrigerator for up to 2 days.

Milk chocolate jelly with red berries

This is a popular dessert in our house. The chocolate jelly has a full, rich chocolate flavour, but it is also very light due to the lack of cream or butter in the recipe. Served with red berries, it is a nice, refreshing dessert that is just as delicious in winter as it is in summer.

For this recipe I use small savarin moulds or aluminium moulds that hold about 100 ml.

■ ■

Serves 6

150 g milk chocolate with 40% cocoa
    mass, e.g. Valrhona's Jiavara,
    see pp. 12–14
4 gelatine leaves
350 ml whole milk

Finely chop the chocolate and tip into a bowl. Soak the gelatine in cold water for 5 minutes.

Bring the milk to the boil. Squeeze the water out of the gelatine leaves and melt completely in the hot milk. Gradually pour one third of the milk over the chocolate, stirring continuously with a spatula to give a smooth, elastic mixture. The mixture will emulsify. When it has become smooth, gradually add the remaining milk, while stirring continuously.

Pour the jelly into the moulds and place in the refrigerator until they set. This takes about 2 hours.

1 vanilla pod
150 g caster sugar
250 ml water
1 star anise
1 stick cinnamon
1 tbsp cornflour blended with 50 ml
   cold water
200 g sweet or sour cherries, stoned
200 g raspberries

Red berries

If you use frozen berries, do not defrost. Pour the hot syrup over them while they are frozen.

Split the vanilla pod lengthways and scrape out the seeds. Put the sugar, water, star anise, cinnamon stick, vanilla pod and seeds in a saucepan and bring to the boil. Stir in the cornflour mixture and allow the syrup to simmer for 2 minutes.

Pour the hot syrup over the cherries. Allow to cool before mixing in the other berries.

Stand in a cool place for a minimum of 2 hours, or overnight. Remove the vanilla pod and cinnamon stick before serving.

Before serving, dip the moulds in a little warm water. Turn the jellies out onto the plates. Serve the jelly with red berries and, if desired, brandy snaps, see p. 170.

The jelly will keep for up to 2 days in the refrigerator.

Chocolate cobblestone

I gave this cake its name because it is the shape of a cobblestone. I ate a similar cake in Paris at my favourite French patisserie, Pierre Hermé. Ginger and chocolate taste fantastic together. In addition to the chocolate and ginger cream, there is a firm almond base to provide texture. If I really want to impress, as I do here, I cover it with dark chocolate icing as in the picture overleaf.

■ ■ ■

1 baking sheet, 30 x 25 cm

90 g almonds
30 g flour
100 g icing sugar
5 egg whites (150 g)
50 g caster sugar

Preheat the oven to 180 °C. In a food processor, grind the almonds with the flour together to make a fine powder. Mix the almond flour with the icing sugar.

Whisk the egg whites and sugar to a stiff meringue. Fold the almond mixture into the meringue with a spatula.

Line a baking sheet with baking parchment and spread the mixture over it in a layer 1.5 cm thick. Bake the base in the centre of the oven for about 20 minutes. Try lifting a corner of the cake base. If it comes away from the baking parchment, the base is ready.

Finished cake bases may be wrapped in cling film and kept in the freezer for up to 1 month.

Chocolate and ginger cream
220 g dark chocolate with 64% cocoa
    mass, see pp. 12–14
1 piece fresh ginger, about 4 cm
50 g caster sugar
250 ml whole milk
300 ml whipping cream (38% fat)
3 egg yolks (60 g)

Finely chop the chocolate and melt in a bain-marie, see p. 19. Peel the ginger and grate finely.

Put the ginger, half the sugar and the milk in a saucepan and bring to the boil.

Beat the egg yolks and the remaining sugar lightly together in a heatproof bowl.

Gradually pour the hot milk over the egg mixture, stirring with a whisk. Then pour the cream back into the saucepan. Get a bowl and a sieve out now, then heat the sauce, while stirring the bottom of the pan with a spatula. It is important to stir continuously to prevent the egg yolks from setting at the bottom of the pan.

When the mixture thickens (85 °C) – with small portions like these this happens very quickly – be ready with the sieve and strain the sauce into the bowl.

Pour the first one third of the sauce into the chocolate and mix with a whisk until smooth and even. Then gradually add the remaining sauce, while stirring continuously.

Stand the chocolate mixture on the worktop to cool to about 35 °C. Whisk the cream, see p. 19. Fold one third of the cream into the chocolate mixture with a spatula. Then fold in the remaining cream.

Assembling:

I use a rectangular cake tin 12 x 17 cm, 5 cm high with a loose base, which I don't use for this recipe. This gives the cake the approximate shape of a cobblestone. You can also use a cake ring 16 cm in diameter and 5 cm high.

Position the mould on a dish covered with baking parchment. Cut the almond base to size and place in the mould. Spoon in the cream and leave in the freezer until the cake is completely frozen. This takes about 4 hours.

Before serving:

Take the cake out of the freezer 4 hours before serving. Warm the mould with a hot, wet tea towel or dip for a few seconds in hot water so the cake comes away a little and the mould can be removed easily.

Put the cake in the refrigerator to defrost. This takes about 3½ hours. Decorate the cake with fresh berries. Use the picture for inspiration.

If I want to make this cake even more special, I ice it with dark chocolate icing. This must be done while it is still frozen. See recipe p. 44. Make the icing and spread it over the cake evenly. Stand it on a wire rack while you ice it. Then put it to defrost as described above.

TIPS
Vanilla sauce can separate if you leave it in the pan while you look for a bowl and sieve. The pan keeps on heating the sauce in the meantime, and hey presto, it has separated.

Milk chocolate mousse

A wonderful, light brown mousse for lovers of milk chocolate, I like to serve it with caramelised almonds. You get plenty of additional texture, and the caramel flavour also filters through well with the mild chocolate.

■ ■

Serves 10

300 g milk chocolate with 40% cocoa
    mass, see pp. 12–14
2 gelatine leaves
1 vanilla pod
250 ml whole milk
3 egg yolks (60 g)
325 ml cream (38% fat)

> Serve with fresh berries, chopped roasted walnuts or chopped cara-melised almonds.

There is no additional sugar in this recipe because of the sweetness of the milk chocolate. However, those with sweet teeth could add a little caster sugar to the eggs.

Finely chop the chocolate and melt in a bain-marie, see p. 19. Soak the gelatine in cold water for at least 5 minutes. Split the vanilla pod lengthways and scrape out the seeds.

Put the milk, vanilla pod and seeds in a saucepan and bring to the boil.

Beat the egg yolks and sugar (if using) lightly together in a heatproof bowl. Gradually pour the hot milk over the eggs, stirring with a whisk. Then pour the cream back into the saucepan. Get your bowl and sieve out now, then heat the sauce, while stirring the bottom of the pan with a wooden spoon. It is important to stir continuously to prevent the egg yolks from setting at the bottom of the pan.

When the mixture thickens (85 °C) – with small portions like these this happens very quickly – be ready with the sieve and strain the sauce into the bowl. Squeeze the water out of the gelatine and melt it in the hot sauce. Mix well.

Pour the first one third of the hot vanilla sauce into the chocolate and mix with a hand whisk until smooth and even. Then gradually add the remaining sauce, while stirring continuously.

Stand the chocolate mixture on the worktop to cool to about 33 °C.

Whisk the cream, see p. 19. Fold one third of the cream into the chocolate mixture with a plastic spatula. Then fold in the remaining cream. Pour the mousse into glasses and stand in the refrigerator until the mousse sets. This takes about 4 hours.

Bittersweet chocolate cream with pastis

Pastis is a drink from the south of France, and I have a great weakness for it. When I was on a summer holiday in Provence a few years ago, I sat in a little café drinking pastis and eating olives, while I waited for my wife to finish her shopping. When she came back, one of the things she had bought was a dark, bitter chocolate from a local chocolatier. I took a bite of the chocolate and washed it down with pastis before I remembered that I was meant to be enjoying an olive instead! However, I sat there savouring this combination for a while, and in fact it was very nice. That is how bittersweet chocolate cream with pastis came about.

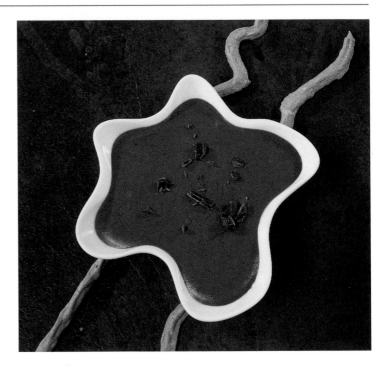

135 g dark chocolate with 64% cocoa
  mass, see pp. 12–14
3 egg yolks (60 g)
50 g caster sugar
40 ml + 230 ml whipping cream
  (38% fat)
4 tbsp pastis, or to taste

Finely chop the chocolate and melt in a bain-marie, see p.19. Put the egg yolks in a heatproof bowl and add the sugar while beating lightly with a whisk.

Bring the 40 ml cream to the boil and pour over the egg yolks, whisking lightly. Pour the melted chocolate into the egg mixture, while stirring with a whisk. Whisk the 230 ml cream until light and creamy, see p. 19.

Wait until the chocolate is lukewarm (40 °C) before folding in the cream with a spatula. Add pastis to taste. Pour the chocolate cream into bowls. It should stand in the refrigerator for 3 hours to set before serving.

Chocolate mousse with caramelised pears

Chocolate, pears, caramel and cognac give an exquisite combination of flavours. I make this dessert in summer and autumn, when the pears are juicy and full of flavour.

■ ■ ■

Serves 8

Caramelised pears

6 pears

lemon juice

300 g sugar

400 ml water

2 tsp butter

4 tbsp cognac

Chocolate mousse

100 g dark chocolate with 70% cocoa
   mass, see pp.12–14

40 g caster sugar

140 ml whole milk

2 egg yolks (40 g)

225 ml whipping cream (38% fat)

Peel and core the pears. Cut in pieces 1 x 1 cm and cover with a little lemon juice and water to stop them turning brown.

Make a light caramel of the sugar with the measured water. Place the pears in it and boil until soft. Remove the pan from the heat and stir in the butter and cognac. Pour the mixture into cocktail glasses.

Finely chop the chocolate and melt in a bain-marie, see p. 19. Put half the sugar in a saucepan with the milk and bring to the boil.

Beat the egg yolks and the remaining sugar together in a heat proof bowl.

Gradually pour the hot milk over the egg mixture while stirring with a whisk. Then pour the cream back into the saucepan. Get your bowl and sieve out now, then heat the sauce, while stirring the bottom of the pan with a spatula. It is important to stir continuously to prevent the egg yolks from setting at the bottom of the pan.

When the mixture thickens (85 °C) – with small portions like these this happens very quickly – be ready with the sieve and strain the sauce into the bowl.

Pour the first one third of the hot custard sauce into the chocolate and mix with a wooden spoon until smooth and even. Then gradually add the remaining sauce, while stirring continuously.

Stand the chocolate mixture on the worktop to cool to about 35 °C.

Whisk the cream, see p. 19. Fold one third of the cream into the chocolate mixture with a spatula. Then fold in the remaining cream.

Pour the mousse into glasses and stand in the refrigerator until the mousse sets. This takes about 4 hours.

Nemi

I was inspired to make this cake after reading the popular Norwegian comic strip about Nemi the Goth girl, who dresses in black and loves chocolate. The cake is dome-shaped and has coal black icing. It is really 'as black as your heart', as Nemi might have said. It has dark chocolate mousse inside and a crisp hazelnut base. Whether or not you are black-hearted, this is a cake to die for.

PS! I won the gold medal for the best taste at an international cake-making competition in Copenhagen with the Nemi cake. I have simplified the recipe for this book, but it is still extremely good. Serve the cake with freshly processed raspberries and vanilla ice cream as accompaniments.

■ ■ ■ ■

Serves 10

For the hazelnut base, see p. 112

Chocolate mousse
190 g dark chocolate, 70% cocoa mass, see pp. 12–14
5 egg yolks (90 g)
45 g caster sugar
40 ml + 350 ml whipping cream (38% fat)

Finely chop the chocolate and melt in a bain-marie, see p. 19. Put the egg yolks in a heatproof bowl and add the sugar while beating gently with a whisk.

Bring the 40 ml cream to the boil and pour over the egg yolks, while whisking gently.

Pour the melted chocolate into the egg mixture, stirring with a whisk.

Whisk the 350 ml cream, see p. 19. Wait until the chocolate becomes lukewarm (40 °C) before folding in the cream with a plastic spatula.

Pour the chocolate mousse into a hemisphere mould that holds about 1 litre, or into small individual moulds holding about 100 ml. I use silicone hemisphere moulds (obtainable from specialist shops) or small muffin tins.

Cut the hazelnut base to size and lay it on top of the mousse. Put in the freezer until it sets. This takes about 4 hours.

4 gelatine leaves
180 g caster sugar
120 g whipping cream (38% fat)
130 ml water
50 g glucose
60 g unsweetened cocoa powder

Black icing

For this icing it is worth having a digital thermometer. The icing has to be heated to 103 °C. then it reaches the right consistency so that with the added gelatine it will cling to the cake.

Soak the gelatine leaves in cold water. Put the remaining ingredients in a saucepan and stir together thoroughly with a whisk. Bring the icing to the boil and keep it boiling while stirring the bottom of the pan continuously with the whisk. It is important to stir constantly to prevent the icing from catching.

When the temperature reaches 103 °C, remove the pan from the heat. If the icing is to cling to the cake, it must be thick enough. I test this by dipping a spoon into the hot icing and putting it in the refrigerator. If the icing slides off the spoon, it is not thick enough; if it clings to the spoon, it will stay on the cake.

Squeeze the water out of the gelatine and let it melt completely in the hot icing. Sieve the icing. Keep the icing warm in a bain-marie, if it is not to be used straight away. If it gets too cold, it should be warmed carefully in a bain-marie or a microwave. Do not let it boil.

Take the frozen mousse out of the mould(s). If using metal moulds, you can dip them for a few seconds in hot water so the mousse will slide out more easily. If you do this, the mousse will have to go back in the freezer for a few minutes so that the outer layer freezes again. This is important because of the icing, which will run off if the outer layer of the mousse has melted. **Note!** If you use silicone moulds, ignore this problem.

Place the frozen mousse on a wire rack and ice it. Leave on a plate to defrost. This takes about 40 minutes for the small ones. The big one takes about 3 hours.

Decorate the cake with fresh berries and macaroons, if desired. Make the macaroons as described on p. 94, but add 2 tsp cocoa powder along with the icing sugar to give you chocolate macaroons.

Chocolate pannacotta

'Panna cotta' means cooked cream in Italian, and this is the key to this dessert, which has a rich velvety consistency. The classic pannacotta has a sweet, mild taste, and is delicious as is but even more so with a little milk chocolate. To freshen it up, I add kesam, which lends the dessert a slightly tart flavour.

■ ■

Serves 10

100 g milk chocolate with 40% cocoa
    mass, e.g. Valrhona's Jiavara,
    see pp. 12–14
1½ gelatine leaves
10 g caster sugar
150 ml whipping cream (38% fat)
130 g kesam 8% (similar to quark or
    fresh curd)
70 g mascarpone

Finely chop the chocolate and tip into a heatproof bowl. Soak the gelatine in cold water for about 5 minutes.

Bring the sugar and cream to the boil. Squeeze the water out of the gelatine and melt completely it in the hot cream. Pour the hot cream over the chocolate and stir together to a smooth mixture.

Mix the kesam and mascarpone in a bowl until smooth, then stir into the chocolate mixture. Pour the pannacotta into bowls and put it to cool in the refrigerator until it sets. This takes about 2 hours.

Serve the pannacotta straight from the refrigerator with fresh berries or a fruit salad. I use strawberries and mangoes with a little sugar.

Chocolate brandy snaps can also be served with this dessert, see p. 170.

White chocolate baskets with fresh berries

This tempting little dish looks impressive and tastes enchanting. The white chocolate cream is rich and sweet. A few raspberries, red currants or other red berries give a fresh sharpness that is a perfect counterbalance for the richness and sweetness. Of course you do not have to make the chocolate baskets. The mousse tastes wonderful without them.

■ ■ ■ ■

Serves 8

White chocolate mousse
200 g white chocolate
2 gelatine leaves
1 vanilla pod
50 ml + 200 ml whipping cream
    (38% fat)
50 ml whole milk
10 g caster sugar
1 egg yolk (20 g)

Finely chop the chocolate. Soak the gelatine in cold water for 5 minutes.

Split the vanilla pod lengthways and scrape out the seeds. Put the vanilla pod and seeds, the 50 ml cream and the milk in a saucepan and bring to the boil.

Beat the egg yolk and sugar lightly together. Gradually pour the hot milk over stirring with a whisk. Then pour the cream sauce back into the saucepan. Get your bowl and sieve out now, then heat the sauce, while stirring the bottom of the pan with a wooden spoon. It is important to stir continuously to prevent the egg yolk from setting at the bottom of the pan.

When the mixture thickens (85 °C) – with small portions like these this happens very quickly – be ready with the sieve and strain the sauce into the bowl.

Squeeze the water out of the gelatine and melt it completely in the hot sauce. Gradually pour the hot sauce over the chopped chocolate while stirring with a spatula. Mix until smooth and even. When the mixture has cooled (30 °C), whisk the 200 ml cream, see p. 19, and fold it into the chocolate mixture.

Pour the mousse into small cake rings 4 cm in diameter and 4 cm deep or muffins tins. Put them in the freezer until the mousse has frozen. This takes about 2 hours.

Put a baking sheet in the freezer at least 2 hours before the dessert is to be served. Take the mousse out 1 hour before serving. Remove the rings and put the dessert in the refrigerator.

Chocolate baskets

150 g dark chocolate

150 g white chocolate

Put a baking sheet in the freezer. Finely chop the chocolate and melt the two kinds separately in a bain-marie or a microwave, see p. 19. To make chocolate baskets, it is important that the chocolate is no more than finger warm (about 33 °C).

Using a spoon, drizzle a small amount of chocolate to form an attractive criss-cross pattern on the chilled baking sheet. It will set quickly. Pour 2 tablespoons of white chocolate over the dark chocolate and spread the white chocolate thinly over the chilled baking sheet, so that you get a sheet of white chocolate with dark chocolate decoration. The chocolate will set quickly. Cut out a rectangle to match the circumference of the mousse and about 1 cm taller. Lift the rectangle of chocolate off the baking sheet and bend it round the mousse. Now put the dessert to defrost in the refrigerator. This takes about 1 hour. Decorate with 200 g assorted red berries before serving, for example, red currants, strawberries and raspberries.

Classic chocolate mousse with egg whites

Dark, strong, soft, delicious, seductive… What is it about this dessert that gives it such enormous appeal? Chocolate mousse is a classic dessert. It must be rich, with a strong chocolate taste, and feel velvety on the tongue. Follow the recipe accurately, bring out the scales and take no chances! That way you will achieve a good result, even on a very bad day.

Serves 10

190 g dark chocolate with 64% cocoa
    mass, see pp. 12–14
80 g crème fraîche
2 egg yolks (40 g)
5 egg whites (150 g)
40 g caster sugar

Finely chop the chocolate and melt in a bain-marie or a microwave, see p. 19. Bring the crème fraîche to the boil and pour over the melted chocolate. Mix well.

Stir the egg yolks into the chocolate mixture with a hand whisk. Beat the mixture together well until smooth and shiny.

Whisk the egg whites and sugar to a meringue. Fold one third of the meringue into the chocolate mixture with a spatula. Then fold in the remainder of the meringue with a spatula.

Pour the chocolate mousse into glasses and place in the refrigerator to cool for 3 hours. The chocolate mousse can be covered well and kept in the refrigerator for up to 2 days.

Chocolate mousse with coffee

There are many people who like chocolate and coffee, and here I have combined the two flavours in a soft, rich mousse. When you mix coffee and chocolate like this, the tastes reinforce one another, resulting in an explosion of flavours.

■

Serves 10

200 g dark chocolate with 64% cocoa
    mass, see pp. 12–14
100 ml whole milk
1 tsp coffee powder
2 egg yolks (40 g)
5 egg whites (150 g)
40 g caster sugar

Finely chop the chocolate and melt in a bain-marie or a microwave, see p. 19.

Bring the milk to the boil. Remove the pan from the heat and stir the coffee powder into the milk with a whisk. Stir the milk into the melted chocolate with a hand whisk. Stir the egg yolks into the chocolate mixture. Beat the mixture together well until smooth and shiny.

Whisk the egg whites and sugar to a meringue. Fold one third of the meringue into the chocolate mixture with a spatula. The fold in the remainder of the meringue with the spatula.

Pour the chocolate mousse into glasses and place in the refrigerator to cool for 3 hours.

The chocolate mousse can be covered well and kept in the refrigerator for up to 2 days.

Meringue cake

Strong, dark chocolate mousse on a crisp nut base and topped with sticks of meringue. What could be more delicious! At the start of his career, a French confectioner and patissier by the name of Gaston Lenôtre made a cake he called La Concorde, inspired by the wonderful Place de la Concorde in Paris. Thirty-five years later the cake is still just as popular, and that is hardly surprising. After having eaten it several times in Paris, I have made my own version inspired by La Concorde.

■ ■ ■

For this cake I used a cake ring 18 cm in diameter and 5 cm high.

Serves 8

Hazelnut base
This base is made without flour. It is extremely good for cakes that have to be gluten-free. Any leftover base can be frozen.

4 egg whites (120 g)
60 g caster sugar
160 g hazelnuts
100 g icing sugar
2 tbsp unsweetened cocoa powder

Preheat the oven to 170 °C. Whisk the egg whites and sugar to a meringue in a foodmixer or by hand.

Roughly chop the hazelnuts in a food processor together with the icing sugar and cocoa. Fold the nut mixture into the meringue with a spatula.

Cover a baking sheet (30 x 25 cm) with baking parchment. With a spatula, spread the mixture over the parchment in a layer 1.5 cm thick.

Bake the base in the centre of the oven for about 25 minutes. Try lifting a corner of the base. If it comes away from the baking parchment, the base is ready. Allow the base to cool on the baking parchment.

Meringue
2 egg whites (60 g)
30 g caster sugar
30 g icing sugar
1 tbsp unsweetened cocoa powder

Preheat the oven to 150 °C. Whisk the egg whites and sugar to a stiff meringue. Sift in the icing sugar and cocoa powder and fold in with a spatula.

Put the meringue mixture in a piping bag with a 5 mm nozzle. Pipe long sticks onto a sheet of baking parchment. Bake the sticks with the oven door ajar until crisp. This takes about 30 minutes. Leave the meringue sticks to cool on a wire rack. Keep in a cake tin in a dry place.

Chocolate mousse

300 g dark chocolate with 64% cocoa
    mass, see pp. 12–14
150 g unsalted butter
3 gelatine leaves
80 ml espresso or strong coffee
4 large egg yolks (100 g)
6 large egg whites (150 g)
100 g caster sugar

Finely chop the chocolate and melt in a bain-marie together with the butter.

Soak the gelatine in cold water for at least 5 minutes.

Make the espresso or strong coffee. Squeeze the water out of the soaked gelatine and melt it completely in the hot coffee.

Stir the egg yolks into the chocolate mixture. Then stir in the hot coffee. Beat the mixture well together with a hand whisk until smooth and shiny.

Whisk the egg whites and sugar to a meringue. Fold one third of the meringue into the chocolate mixture with a spatula. Then fold in the remaining meringue with the spatula.

Assembling:
Brush the inside of the cake ring with a little neutral oil, for example sunflower or soya oil. This is to make it easier to get the cake out of the ring.

Put the cake ring on a flat plate. Break or cut out a piece of hazelnut base and lay it in the bottom of the cake ring. Cover with chocolate mousse.

Put the cake in the freezer overnight or until completely frozen. This takes about 4 hours. If well wrapped, the cake can be kept in the freezer for 14 days.

Before serving:
Warm the cake ring with a hot damp towel or similar so the ring comes away easily. Remove the cake ring and put the cake in the refrigerator to defrost. This takes about 4 hours.

Break the meringue sticks into shorter pieces and cover the cake with them. If desired, the cake may also be sprinkled with cocoa or icing sugar before serving.

Chocolat crémeux with citrus liqueur

Chocolat crémeux is a blend of chocolate mousse and chocolate cream. It has both the sharp, bitter chocolate taste of a mousse and the softness and richness that are characteristic of cream. I have added citrus liqueur, as the citric acid counterbalances the bitterness of chocolate particularly well.

For this dessert I use small silicone or aluminium moulds holding 100 ml.

■ ■

Serves 8

100 g dark chocolate with 64% cocoa
  mass, see pp. 12–14
125 g crème fraîche
3 egg yolks (40 g)
30 g caster sugar
2 tbsp citrus liqueur
150 ml whipping cream (38% fat)

Finely chop the chocolate and melt in a bain-marie, see p. 19.

Put the crème fraîche in a saucepan and bring to the boil. Beat the egg yolks and sugar together lightly in a heatproof bowl. Gradually pour the hot crème fraîche over the egg mixture while stirring with a whisk.

Pour the first one third of the hot egg mixture into the chocolate and stir with a whisk until the mixture is smooth and even. Then gradually add the remaining mixture, stirring continuously. Add citrus liqueur to taste.

Stand the chocolate mixture on the worktop to cool until lukewarm, about 35 °C.

Whisk the cream, see p. 19. Fold one third of the cream into the chocolate mixture with a spatula. Then fold in the rest of the cream.

Spoon the chocolat crémeux into individual moulds and stand in the freezer until set firm. This takes about 2 hours.

You can also serve it in glasses. Stand in the refrigerator until set. This takes about 2 hours.

Take the creams out of the freezer 1 hour before serving and remove the moulds. Put them on plates to defrost. Serve with chocolate sauce.

Chocolate sauce
100 g chocolate with 66% cocoa mass,
  see pp. 12–14
100 ml whole milk
25 g caster sugar

Finely chop the chocolate and tip into a heatproof bowl. Bring the milk and sugar to the boil. Remove from the heat and gradually pour over the chocolate while stirring with a whisk. Serve the sauce warm.

You could also make chocolate decorations, see p. 175.

White chocolate mousse with grapefruit sauce

The idea for this dessert came from a gin and tonic. It was the Swedish confectioner Jan Hedh who introduced me to this dessert. The grapefruit sauce flavoured with gin is reminiscent of the refreshing drink. The white chocolate mousse is rich and sweet and the sauce adds the sharp freshness and bitterness. Small pieces of baked filo pastry give the dessert a little body. This is a very nice, mild, light summer dessert.

■ ■

Serves 8

White chocolate mousse
200 g white chocolate
100 ml milk
1 gelatine leaf
2 egg yolks (40 g)
3 egg whites (90 g)
20 g caster sugar

Finely chop the chocolate and melt in a bain-marie, see p. 19.

Soak the gelatine in cold water for at least 5 minutes. Bring the milk to the boil, and remove the pan from the heat. Squeeze the water out of the soaked gelatine and melt it completely in the hot milk.

Pour the hot milk over the chocolate and beat together with a hand whisk. Stir in the egg yolks. Leave the mixture to cool until lukewarm.

Whisk the egg whites and sugar to a meringue. Fold one third of the meringue into the chocolate mixture with a spatula. Then fold in the rest.

Pour the mousse into glasses and place in the refrigerator to set. This takes about 2 hours.

Grapefruit sauce
2–3 large pink grapefruit
30 g caster sugar
1 tsp cornflour mixed with 1 tbsp cold
    water
2 tsp gin

Peel one grapefruit and cut out the segments between the natural divisions, discarding the membrane. After cutting out the flesh, squeeze the juice out of what is left. Divide the second grapefruit in two and squeeze out the juice. That should give about 200 ml grapefruit juice, but you may need the third!

Bring the grapefruit juice and sugar to the boil. Whisk in the cornflour mixture. Simmer the mixture for about ½ minute. Set the sauce aside to cool. Add gin to taste when the sauce is cold.

Lay the grapefruit segments on top of the mousse. Pour a little sauce over them and, if desired, serve with caramelised filo pastry, see next page, or tuile biscuits, see p. 171.

Caramelised filo pastry

Filo pastry

Melted butter

Icing sugar

Preheat the oven to 200 °C. Take a sheet of filo pastry and brush it with butter. Dust lightly with icing sugar. Lay another sheet of filo on top and press the sheets gently together. Brush the upper side with butter and dust with icing sugar. Bake the double sheet of filo in the oven until it is golden and the sugar has caramelised. This takes 2–3 minutes. Allow the filo to cool and break in pieces.

Chocolate cream with raspberry terrine

In the 17th century, chocolate was both exotic and cloaked in mystery. It was credited with many positive attributes and was even used as a medicine, but it was also the subject of superstition. An example of this can be found in a letter that the Marquise de Sévigné, famous for her witty correspondence describing life at the court of Louis XIV, wrote to her daughter in 1671: 'The Marquise de Coëtlogon drank so much chocolate when pregnant last year that she gave birth to a boy as black as the devil.' The lady in question was living on her husband's plantation in South America at the time. He was so dismayed that he banned the drinking of chocolate on the plantation to avoid this happening again. I wonder if he also forbade his wife to meet the slaves on the plantation?

I think this dessert is an example of the magical properties of chocolate. Thick dark chocolate cream that melts in the mouth combines perfectly with the sweet and powerful flavours of the berries in the red raspberry terrine.

■ ■ ■

Serves 8

Raspberry terrine
3½ gelatine leaves
440 g raspberries
60 g caster sugar

Chocolate cream
180 g dark chocolate with 64% cocoa
    mass, e.g. Valrhona's Manjari,
    see pp. 3 egg yolks (60 g)
70 g caster sugar
200 ml whipping cream (38% fat)
180 ml whole milk

To serve:
100 g assorted berries, e.g. raspberries,
    blueberries, wild strawberries,
    strawberries

Soak the gelatine in cold water for 5 minutes. Run the raspberries through a food processor or mash with a hand-held mixer and strain out the pips. Measure the result – you should have 150 ml purée.

In a saucepan, bring half the purée with the sugar to the boil. Remove the pan from the heat. Squeeze the water out of the gelatine and melt it in the hot raspberry mixture. Stir in the rest of the purée and mix well. Line a loaf tin with baking parchment. Pour the raspberry purée into the tin to form a layer about 1 cm thick. Put in the freezer until it sets hard.

Finely chop the chocolate. In a heatproof bowl, beat the egg yolks and sugar together lightly. Bring the cream and milk to the boil. Gradually pour the hot milk over the egg mixture while stirring with a whisk. Then pour the cream back into the saucepan.

Have your bowl and sieve ready to strain the cream. Heat the cream, while stirring the bottom of the pan with a spatula. It is important to stir continuously to prevent the egg yolks from setting at the bottom of the pan. When the mixture thickens (85 °C), strain it into a bowl. Gradually pour the hot sauce over the chocolate, stirring in small circles with a spatula. Stir the mixture with a hand-held mixer to blend it properly.

The cream is now quite fluid. Set it to cool overnight in the refrigerator in order to set. If the cream is to be served on the day it is made, I recommend the chocolate cream described on p. 61, leaving out the Calvados. The chocolate cream in the present recipe must be made the day before. You may feel this is inconvenient, but the velvety smooth consistency you will achieve this way is definitely worth waiting a day for.

Cut slices of the frozen raspberry terrine and put on the plates to defrost. Use a spoon dipped in hot water to shape the chocolate cream into balls. Place two balls on each plate. Decorate with fresh berries.

The chocolate cream may be served with chocolate tuile biscuits, see p. 171.

Chocolate foam with vanilla ice cream

In the old days a cream-whipper with gas cartridges would come into its own for this recipe but today we have little battery-operated gadgets that do a fair job of creating foam very quickly, or you may have one of those coffee machines that will also make cappuccinos with their foam. Here I have made a milk chocolate foam. Spray it into bowls and serve with vanilla ice cream.

Chocolate foam

100 g dark chocolate with 56% cocoa
   mass, e. g. Valrhona's Caraque,
   see pp. 12–14
5 egg whites (150 g)

Finely chop the chocolate and melt in a bain-marie, see p. 19. Put the egg whites in the melted chocolate and beat together thoroughly with a hand whisk, then whizz with the foam-maker.

Fill a saucepan with water. The water should be the same depth as the height of the mixture in the bottle. Heat the water to 76 °C. Use a thermometer to be certain. Put the bottle in the water and leave it there for about 5 minutes. Remove it from the water and leave to cool at room temperature or cool in cold water until it is lukewarm. It is important that the mixture should be lukewarm and not too cold when it is to be used. Put in two gas cartridges. Shake well. Spray the mixture out into deep bowls.

Serve the foam immediately with a ball of vanilla ice cream and, if desired, some crispy fried pastry, see p. 173, or a biscuit.

White chocolate mousse with raspberry terrine

This is a nice light summer dessert, which I make when the raspberries begin to ripen. The sweet, mild chocolate mousse is the perfect base for a little fresh, sharp raspberry terrine.

■ ■ ■

Raspberry terrine, see recipe on page 148

White chocolate mousse
200 g white chocolate
2 gelatine leaves
1 vanilla pod, or to taste
50 ml + 200 ml whipping cream
150 ml whole milk
10 g caster sugar
1 egg yolk (20 g)

Finely chop the chocolate. Soak the gelatine in cold water for about 5 minutes.

Split the vanilla pod lengthways and scrape out the seeds. Put the vanilla pod and seeds, 50 ml cream and the milk in a saucepan and bring to the boil.

Beat the egg yolk and sugar lightly together. Gradually pour the hot milk over the egg mixture, stirring with a whisk. Then pour the custard sauce back into the saucepan. Get your bowl and a sieve out now, then heat the sauce, while stirring the bottom of the pan with a wooden spoon. It is important to stir continuously to prevent the egg yolk from setting at the bottom of the pan.

When the mixture thickens (85 °C) – with small portions like these this happens very quickly – be ready with the sieve and strain the sauce into the bowl.

Squeeze the water out of the gelatine and melt it completely in the hot sauce. Gradually pour the hot sauce over the chopped chocolate while stirring with a spatula. Mix until smooth and even.

When the mixture has cooled (30 °C), whip the cream (to a cream), see p. 19, and fold it into the chocolate mixture. Leave the mousse in the bowl and stand in the refrigerator until it sets. This takes about 3 hours.

To serve:
Take the raspberry terrine out of the freezer and cut in 2 cm squares. Use a teaspoon dipped in warm water to make balls of mousse. The mousse can be served on a tuile biscuit, see p.171, and garnished with fresh raspberries.

Chocolate cream with sugar foam and baked pineapple

El Bulli is a famous experimental Spanish restaurant, and they are trendsetters in both sweet and savoury cuisine. I came across this sugar foam or 'cloud', as they call it, and was deeply fascinated. It works incredibly well as a light, sweet accompaniment to dark chocolate cream and fresh pineapple.

■ ■ ■

Serves 8

Chocolate cream
130 g dark chocolate with 66% cocoa mass, see pp. 12–14
3 egg yolks (60 g)
30 g caster sugar
40 ml + 230 ml whipping cream (38% fat)

Finely chop the chocolate and melt in a bain-marie, see p. 19.

Put the egg yolks in a heatproof bowl and add the sugar while beating lightly with a whisk.

Bring the 40 ml cream to the boil and pour it over the egg yolks while whisking lightly.

Tip the melted chocolate into the egg mixture while stirring with a whisk.

Whisk the 230 ml cream until light and creamy, see p. 19. Wait until the chocolate mixture is lukewarm (40 °C) before folding in the cream with a spatula.

Pour the chocolate cream into individual moulds and freeze it. This takes about 2 hours.

Baked pineapple
1 pineapple, about 1 kg before peeling
1 vanilla pod
100 g caster sugar
100 ml orange juice
1 orange
2 fresh apricots

Preheat the oven to 220 °C. Peel the pineapple and cut in half lengthways. Remove the core and discard it. Cut the pineapple flesh in chunks 2 x 2 cm.

Split the vanilla pod lengthways and scrape out the seeds. Put the vanilla pod, seeds, sugar and orange juice in a saucepan and bring to the boil.

Place the pineapple chunks in an ovenproof dish and pour the hot syrup over them. Bake the pineapple in the oven until it begins to brown. This takes about 30 minutes. Turn the chunks 2–3 times during baking. Stand them to cool at room temperature.

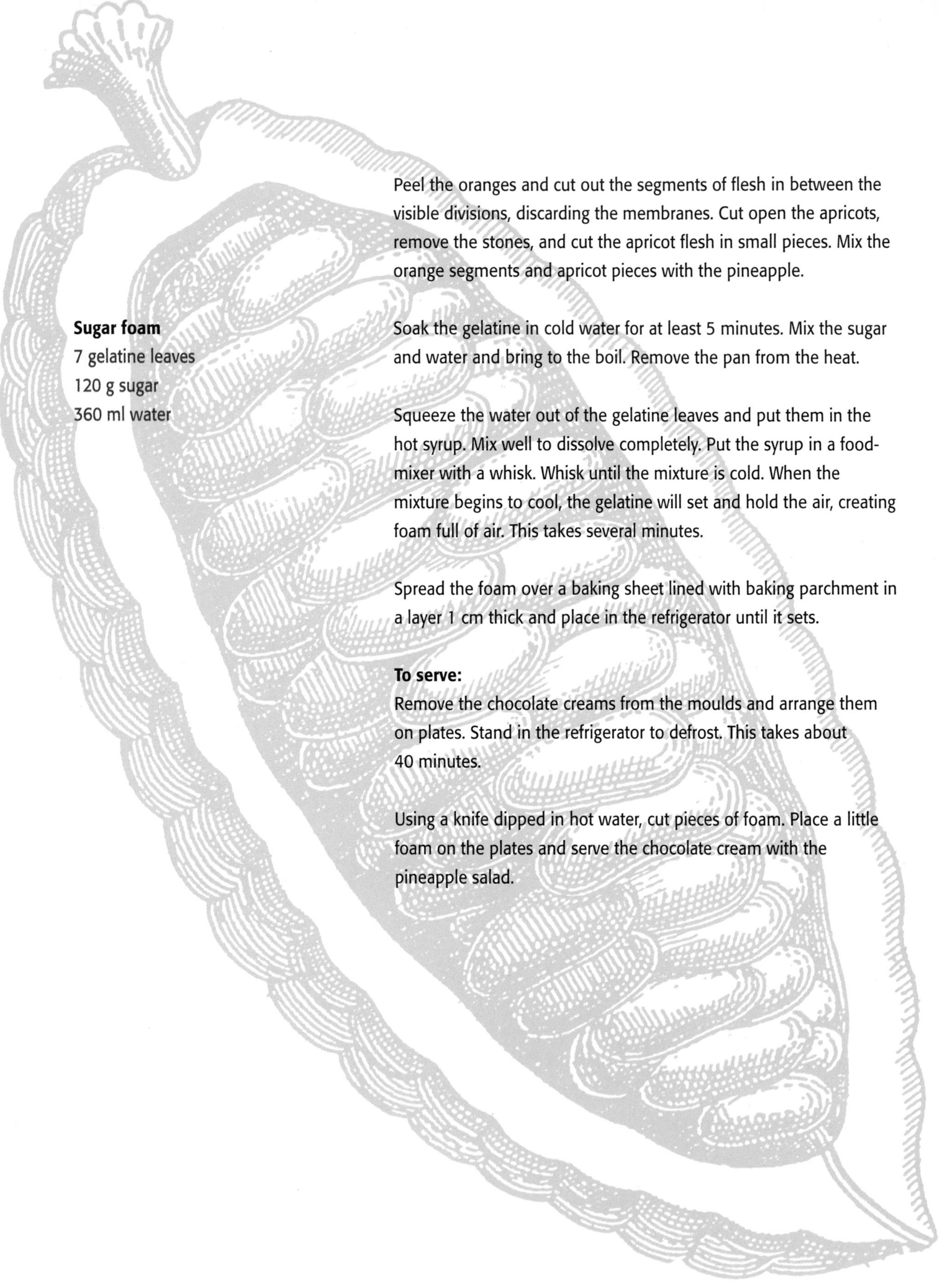

Peel the oranges and cut out the segments of flesh in between the visible divisions, discarding the membranes. Cut open the apricots, remove the stones, and cut the apricot flesh in small pieces. Mix the orange segments and apricot pieces with the pineapple.

Sugar foam
7 gelatine leaves
120 g sugar
360 ml water

Soak the gelatine in cold water for at least 5 minutes. Mix the sugar and water and bring to the boil. Remove the pan from the heat.

Squeeze the water out of the gelatine leaves and put them in the hot syrup. Mix well to dissolve completely. Put the syrup in a food-mixer with a whisk. Whisk until the mixture is cold. When the mixture begins to cool, the gelatine will set and hold the air, creating foam full of air. This takes several minutes.

Spread the foam over a baking sheet lined with baking parchment in a layer 1 cm thick and place in the refrigerator until it sets.

To serve:
Remove the chocolate creams from the moulds and arrange them on plates. Stand in the refrigerator to defrost. This takes about 40 minutes.

Using a knife dipped in hot water, cut pieces of foam. Place a little foam on the plates and serve the chocolate cream with the pineapple salad.

Chocolate savarins with chilli

Savarin is the name of a cake, but it is also the name of the shape of the mould. What we have here is not the classic savarin cake but the shape, and it is filled with a thick chocolate cream flavoured with chilli. In the 18th century, they added chilli to the chocolate to heat the blood and thereby increase passion. They believed firmly in this mixture as an aphrodisiac. And who is to say it does not work?

■ ■ ■

Serves 12

If you do not have any savarin moulds, use individual moulds holding about 100 ml.

Chocolate Savarins
200 g dark chocolate with 64% cocoa mass, see pp. 12–14
60 g caster sugar
250 ml whole milk
4 cm fresh chilli, deseeded and roughly
3 egg yolks (70 g)
300 ml whipping cream (38% fat)

Finely chop the chocolate and melt in a bain-marie, see p. 19.

Put half the sugar, the milk and the chilli in a saucepan and bring to the boil.

Beat the egg yolks and the rest of the sugar lightly together in an ovenproof bowl. Gradually pour the hot milk over the egg mixture, stirring with a whisk. Then pour the cream back into the saucepan. Get a bowl and a sieve out now, then heat the sauce, while stirring the bottom of the pan with a spatula. It is important to stir continuously to prevent the egg yolk from setting at the bottom of the pan.

When the mixture thickens (85 °C) – with such small portions this happens very quickly – be ready with the sieve and strain the sauce into the bowl.

Pour the first one third of the hot sauce into the chocolate and mix with a spatula until smooth and even. Then gradually add the remaining sauce, while stirring continuously.

Stand the chocolate mixture on the worktop to cool to about 35 °C.

Whisk the cream, see p. 19. Fold one third of the cream into the chocolate mixture with a spatula. Then fold in the remaining cream.

Pour the chocolate cream into glasses and stand in the refrigerator until the cream is completely frozen. This takes about 24 hours.

Take the cream out of the refrigerator and arrange on plates to de-

Pastry base

300 g flour

200 g unsalted butter in 2 cm (¾ in.)
cubes

100 g icing sugar

1 egg

frost. Serve with fresh berries. I usually serve this cream on a pastry base.

If there is any pastry left over, it can be wrapped in plastic and kept for up to 3 weeks in the freezer. This recipe makes 650 g dough.

Rub the flour, icing sugar and butter together in a bowl by hand or in a foodmixer.

Add the egg and knead into a dough or mix together quickly in a foodmixer until the dough just comes together.

Wrap the dough in clingfilm and leave in the refrigerator for at least 2 hours.

Roll the dough out to a thickness of 2 mm and cut out rounds of a diameter a little larger than the individual moulds. Put them in the refrigerator for about 1 hour before baking them in a preheated oven at 170 °C.

An easier version:

Pour the chocolate cream into cocktail glasses and stand them in the refrigerator to set. You will not have to wait for them to freeze before removing them from the moulds. If desired, serve with biscuits on the side.

Three savoury dishes

Most of us connect chocolate with cakes, ices, desserts and confectionery, and we usually consume chocolate in this way too. In South America, on the other hand, they use chocolate to flavour savoury dishes. In southern Europe it is also more common to have chocolate in first or main courses and not just in desserts. However, we are not talking thick, sweet chocolate sauces but a small amount of chocolate with a low sugar content that gives a sauce just a hint of the characteristic chocolate flavour. I really enjoy using chocolate as a savoury dinner ingredient, and this section features recipes for three main dishes with chocolate, both white and dark.

Scampi with mushroom and cucumber ragout and chocolate sauce

Shellfish such as scampi and lobster have a sweetness that goes very well with bitter chocolate. If you have read the book Chocolat or seen the film, you will probably recognise this recipe from the big birthday party. In this story, the reluctant guests, who originally boycotted chocolate because they were afraid of the priest and the wrath of God, are carried away by the food and the atmosphere. They are uplifted to a happier and more generous plane. Good food, prepared with love, often has that effect on a party.

Serves 4

8 fresh scampi
frying oil
3 cm fresh chilli, chopped approx.
   30 g each of carrots, celeriac, onions,
   and leeks, all chopped
2 tbsp tomato purée
2 tbsp cold unsalted butter
20 g dark chocolate with 60–70%
   cocoa mass, see pp. 12–14
salt and pepper

Remove the heads from the scampi and peel the tails. Run the tip of a sharp knife along the back and remove the black intestine. Rinse and set the tails aside. Collect the heads and shells in a bag and crush with a rolling pin.

Heat a little oil in a saucepan until smoking hot. Add the crushed shells and fry for 2–3 minutes.

Add the chilli, the other vegetables and the tomato purée and fry for about 2 minutes. Then add sufficient water to cover the shells and simmer for about 20 minutes.

Remove from the heat, strain off the solids and discard. If necessary, return the pan to the heat to reduce the liquid to about one third. Off the heat, stir in the butter to thicken the sauce. Stir in the chocolate and season with salt and pepper.

Mushroom and cucumber ragout
½ cucumber
50 g shitake or oyster mushrooms
frying oil
butter
salt and pepper

Peel the cucumber, scrape out the seeds with a spoon and cut in pieces.

Fry the mushrooms in oil. Add a little butter at the end of the frying time. Season with salt and pepper. Keep warm and stir in the cucumber immediately before serving.

Season the scampi with salt and pepper. Fry the tails in oil in a hot pan for 1–2 minutes then remove from the fat with a slotted spoon and drain on kitchen paper.

Arrange the scampi tails on the ragout and spoon on some sauce.

Turbot with grapefruit and white chocolate beurre blanc.

In butter sauces, a little acid in the form of wine is often used to counterbalance the fat. In this sauce I have added wine and grapefruit, which also gives the sauce a touch of bitterness. It is important to counterbalance this with a suitable dash of sweetness. People usually add sugar or honey, but here I have used white chocolate. It makes an extremely good sauce that goes perfectly with the 'king of the sea'.

Serves 4

Pickled red onion

¼ red onion, cut In small segments
1 tbsp sugar
4 tbsp red wine vinegar
500 ml water
olive oil

Fry the onion in oil until transparent. Add the other ingredients and bring to the boil. Set aside to cool.

Sautéed spring cabbage

½ small spring cabbage
2 shallots, finely chopped
1 tbsp butter
salt and pepper
olive oil

Heat a little oil in a pan and fry the shallots until transparent. Add the cabbage and sauté it (= fry without browning). Stir in the butter and season with salt and pepper.

Grapefruit and white chocolate beurre blanc

2 grapefruit
1 shallot, finely chopped
100 ml white wine
50 ml whipping cream (38% fat)
30 g white chocolate, finely chopped
100 g cold unsalted butter, in cubes
juice of ¼ lemon
salt and pepper

Cut the segments of flesh out of one of the grapefruit, discarding any membrane, and cut them in two. Squeeze the juice out of the leftover parts of the grapefruit and the second grapefruit.

Fry the shallot in the oil until transparent. Add the wine and grapefruit juice. Boil and reduce until the liquid has almost disappeared. Add the cream and bring to the boil. Remove the pan from the heat.

Stir in the chocolate and butter until it has all melted. Season with lemon juice, salt and pepper. PS! Do not boil the sauce after the butter has been added or it will separate. Add the grapefruit segments just before serving.

Divide the turbot up to give four helpings. Season with salt and

Turbot

800 g turbot fillets
salt and pepper
olive oil
butter

pepper. Pan-fry the fish over medium heat in equal parts of oil and butter. Fry on both sides.

Turbot sausages

If you have off-cuts of fish and want to make something extra with them:

200 g turbot flesh
2 eggs
100 ml whipping cream (38% fat)
salt, pepper and cayenne pepper
sausage skin

Blend the turbot and egg together in a food processor. Dilute with cold cream. Season with salt, pepper and cayenne. Fill the sausage skin with the 'sausage meat', using a piping bag or a sausage-filler. Knot to make small sausages about 3 cm (1¼ in.) long. Make two small cuts in each sausage and fry together with the turbot fillets.

Venison with chocolate sauce

I created this dish for a romantic dinner with my wife on our honeymoon. We had rented a flat in Paris with a well-appointed kitchen, precisely with relaxed candle-lit dinners, good food and plenty of wine in mind. Early in the morning, we went to the market, where we got our hands on some venison. Later the same day, I bought some chocolate, which was intended for dessert. In a flash of inspiration I saw a vision of flavours combining game, which has a slightly stronger taste than beef, and dark bitter chocolate. No sooner thought than done, and my wife and I were both very pleased with the result. It is a good idea to serve this dish by candlelight.

Serves 4

Fondant potatoes
4 large potatoes
200 g butter
salt and pepper

Preheat the oven to 225 °C. Peel the potatoes and cut in thick slices. If desired, you could use a round pastry cutter to cut them out, as in the picture. Season the potato slices with salt and pepper and place in an ovenproof dish together with the butter. Bake in the oven for about 40 minutes until soft. Baste the potatoes with the butter at regular intervals.

Savoy cabbage
1 small savoy
Butter
1 shallot, finely chopped
½ clove garlic, finely chopped
Salt and pepper

Separate the cabbage leaves and discard the outer leaves. You will need about 8 leaves. Boil the cabbage in water with sea salt for 4 minutes, then cool immediately in cold water. Remove the leaves, dry them and cut out the hard centres and stalks. Cut the remainder in strips. Fry in butter together with the shallot and garlic. Season with salt and pepper.

Apricot and chilli chutney
4 fresh apricots
2 tbsp olive oil
3 cm chilli, and finely chopped
1 tsp sugar
½ tsp butter
Salt

Roughly chop the apricot flesh and fry in oil with the chilli. Add the sugar and simmer to make a compote. Season with butter and salt.

Chocolate and Parmesan crisps
50 g Parmesan
1 tsp chopped dark chocolate

Preheat the oven to 170 °C. Grate the Parmesan and sprinkle onto baking parchment in a thin layer. Sprinkle chocolate on top and bake the cheese until golden. Allow to cool and break in pieces.

800 g venison fillet

salt and pepper

crushed juniper berries

thyme

butter

oil

1 shallot, roughly chopped

1 small carrot, roughly chopped

1 clove garlic, roughly chopped

1 tbsp sherry vinegar

100 ml white wine

100 ml beef stock

1 tbsp raspberries

2 tsp sugar

40 g unsalted butter in cubes

20 g dark chocolate with 70% cocoa
mass, finely chopped

Leave the meat to stand at room temperature for 2 hours before cooking. Preheat the oven to 170 °C.

Season the meat with salt, pepper, juniper berries and thyme. Brown the venison in a deep frying pan with equal quantities of butter and oil. Gradually add the vegetables.

Remove the meat from the pan and pour in the sherry vinegar, wine, stock, raspberries and sugar. Scrape the bottom of the pan well with a wooden spoon. Simmer for about 15 minutes. Sieve the juice and reduce until you have about 50 ml sauce. Remove the pan from the heat. Bring the sauce back to the boil immediately before serving and stir in the butter and chocolate. PS! Do not boil this sauce after the butter has been added or it will separate.

Roast the meat in the oven at intervals of 3 minutes x 5. The meat must rest for 5 minutes each time. Let the meat rest wrapped in aluminium foil for about 10 minutes before carving.

Fried mushrooms

200 g assorted wild mushrooms, e.g.
chanterelles and boletus, cleaned

butter

1 clove garlic, finely chopped

1 shallot, finely chopped

chives, finely chopped

salt and pepper

Cut the mushrooms into suitably sized pieces. Fry in butter over medium heat. Season with salt and pepper. Add the garlic, shallot and chives at the end of the cooking time.

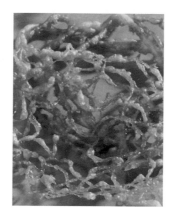

Trimmings

Brandy snaps

These little caramel biscuits are nice and crisp and sweet. I often use them to decorate creams, mousses, ices and parfaits.

80 g caster sugar
80 g unsalted butter
4 tbsp flour
1 tbsp glucose or light honey
1 tsp cocoa powder, (optional)

Preheat the oven to 180 °C. Line a baking sheet with baking parchment.

Mix all the ingredients together thoroughly in a small bowl.

Using a teaspoon, place small blobs of mixture about 1 cm in diameter on the baking parchment. Make sure you leave a 5-cm space between them, as they will expand. If you want to make them tubular, use a bit more mixture, about a teaspoonful, so they will be bigger. Bake the biscuits in the centre of the oven for about 3 minutes until golden. Leave them to cool on the baking sheet.

When the snaps are newly baked and soft, they can be shaped. Leave them on the baking sheet until they just begin to set. Then, very swiftly, roll them round the handle of a wooden spoon or similar and form tubes, or lay them over small cups to make curves. If they get too hard and break, you can put them back in the oven until they soften up again.

> If you plan to make the snaps with chocolate, it is a good idea to keep back a little of the dough to make a pale snap. It can be difficult to tell when the chocolate ones are ready because they are so dark. If baked with a pale one, you can use that as an indicator.

Tuile biscuits

These biscuits may be eaten on their own, but they also make a very good accompaniment to cakes and desserts.

Preheat the oven to 180 °C. Mix all the ingredients in a bowl and stir to a smooth mixture with a hand whisk.

I usually cut stencils out of cardboard, for example squares or rounds, and spread the mixture over the stencil. When I remove the stencil sheet, a perfect round or square is left behind on the baking sheet.

Bake the biscuits in the centre of the oven for about 3 minutes until golden. Leave the biscuits to cool on the baking sheet.

When the biscuits are newly baked and straight from the oven, they can be bent and shaped easily. Leave them on the baking sheet until they just begin to set. For ices, I roll them round a cornet mould. For other shapes, bend them over wooden handles, thin rolling pins, cups, or anything suitable in your kitchen.

NB! Before the cakes are baked, they may be sprinkled with chopped almonds and various kinds of seeds.

50 g icing sugar
50 g flour
2 egg whites (50 g)
50 g butter, at room temperature

Chocolate tuiles
Same as for tuile biscuits, but add 1 tsp unsweetened cocoa powder.

If you plan to make chocolate tuiles, it is a good idea to keep back a little of the dough before mixing in the powder. It is easier to see when the pale biscuit is ready than with the dark chocolate biscuits.

Chocolate caramel flake

This decoration adds extra texture to desserts and cakes

80 g dark chocolate
200 g sugar (preferably cane sugar)
100 ml water
200 g glucose

Preheat the oven to 180 °C. Finely chop the chocolate.

Mix the sugar and water in a saucepan. Bring to the boil and continue boiling for 1 minute until the sugar has dissolved. Add the glucose. Heat the mixture to 158 °C. Take a little of the syrup and put it on a plate. It should set and go hard. The sugar must not go brown. That means it is too hot.

Remove the pan from the heat and stir in the chocolate. Pour the mixture out onto a silicone non-stick liner or a sheet of baking parchment. Lay another non-stick liner or sheet of parchment on top and roll out thinly with a rolling pin. Remove the upper cover and put the mixture in the oven for half a minute.

Remove the baking sheet and pull out pieces of caramel. If it is too hot and runny, let it cool a little. It should be sufficiently elastic for you to stretch it out in thin flakes. If it hardens, put it back in the oven for a while.

Crispy fried pastry

2 egg whites (60 g)
20 g icing sugar
20 g flour
40 g cornflour

500 ml sunflower oil for frying

Mix all the ingredients together thoroughly. Leave the batter to stand and rise for at least 8 hours, preferably overnight.

Fill a small saucepan half full of oil and heat to 180 °C. Check the temperature of the oil with a thermometer. If you do not have one, you can put a dry wooden spoon in the oil. When it begins to bubble away from the wood, the oil is hot enough.

Spoon the mixture into a small plastic bag. Cut a 1–2 mm opening at the corner of the bag. Squeeze the mixture down into the oil in small rings. Cook in the oil until golden. Make sure you turn them during cooking. Take them out with a slotted spoon and put them to drain on kitchen paper.

Sugar spirals

250 g sugar (preferably cane sugar)
100 ml water
100 g glucose

Stir the sugar and water in a saucepan. Bring to the boil and continue boiling for 1 minute until the sugar has dissolved.

Add the glucose. Heat the mixture to 160 °C. As a test, you can take a little of the syrup and put it on a plate. It should set and go hard. The sugar must not go brown. That means it is too hot.

Leave the sugar to cool until it begins to be elastic. Put a little oil on a sharpening stone or similar. When the sugar is elastic enough to be pulled out, take some of the mixture on a spoon and wind it round a wooden spoon handle or a sharpening stone. It will set quickly.

If the mixture in the saucepan goes hard, warm it up carefully again. Keep the sugar in a dry place at room temperature.

You can make caramel spirals by boiling the sugar a little longer until it goes a pale caramel colour.

Chocolate trimmings

These chocolate decorations are made with tempered chocolate. Tempering chocolate is a bit tedious, but it is not difficult. Buy a digital thermometer and follow the instructions precisely and you will achieve superb results, see p. 14. It is a good idea to make a lot of trimmings when you first get started. Put them in an airtight container and keep at room temperature. They will keep for many weeks.

Chocolate flake

Tempered chocolate can be spread thinly over OHP film or an acetate sheet, or baking parchment. You can also sprinkle it with grated chocolate. Put the chocolate in the refrigerator for 1 minute. Take it out again and leave at room temperature for 30 minutes. Break it in pieces when it has set and use for decoration.

Chocolate trellis

This can be made with dark, milk or white chocolate. Cut baking parchment in pieces 10 x 15 cm. Temper the chocolate and spoon into a small plastic bag or a cone of baking parchment. Cut a small hole in the bag and pipe a trellis over the paper. Roll the paper up and place in the refrigerator for 1 minute. Take it out again and leave at room temperature for 30 minutes. Remove the paper carefully.

Chocolate curls

These can be made with dark, milk or white chocolate. Cut OHP film or an acetate sheet in strips 4 x 20 cm. Temper the chocolate and spoon into a small plastic bag or a cone of baking parchment. Cut a small hole in the bag and pipe stripes along the OHP film. Roll it round once in a spiral and put something heavy on the ends to prevent them from springing open. Place in the refrigerator for 1 minute. Take it out again and leave at room temperature for 30 minutes. Remove the plastic carefully.

Imperial Measurements

Sverre Sætre has calculated the proportions of the ingredients down to the last gram. You are recommended to use the metric measurements, as conversions are likely to result in inaccurate approximations or strange fractions of ounces etc. For those of you who would still like to use Imperial measurements, the following methods of calculating the conversions are offered below.

To convert Centigrade (Celsius) to Fahrenheit: Multiply the number of degrees °C by 9, divide by 5, and add 32.

To convert grams to ounces, divide the number of grams by 28.35

To convert millilitres to fluid ounces, divide the number of ml by 30.

To convert centimetres to inches, divide the number of cm by 2.54.